The Star Crossed Serpent

Volume I

"*Fire as such is the province of the Alder (tree), the God of the Underworld - Time* - that which creates and destroys the world of appearances - finally Bran or Brian/Baal, the God of Fire, of Craft, of lower magic and fertility and death. All things that are of this world belong to him, the Star-Crossed Serpent. So you come to *the true meaning of the cauldron. Bring forth the star-son, and you have Dionysus, the horn child and Jesus Christ in one.*" - Robert Cochrane

The Star Crossed Serpent
Volume I - Origins:
Evan John Jones 1966-1998

The Legend of Tubal Cain
by
Evan John Jones
&
Shani Oates

Edited and annotated by Shani Oates,
Additional material by Robert Cochrane. 'Cain:
an Agricultural Myth' by kind permission of
the author, Robin-theDart (Martinmas 2010)

Published by
Mandrake of Oxford
PO Box 250
OXFORD
OX1 1AP (UK)

Other books by Shani Oates and available from Mandrake:
*Tubelo's Green Fire: Mythos, Ethos, Female, Male and Priestly Mysteries of The
Clan of Tubal Cain*, isbn 978-1-906958-07-7

*The Arcane Veil: Witchcraft and Occult Science from the People of the Dark-ages
to the People of Goda, of the Clan of Tubal Cain.*
978-1-906958-35-0 (£25/$40 hbk)

For Val

Sketch of John -   Halcyon Days

6

Contents

Preface

This book has been a long time coming to fruition. Twelve years ago, I had the privilege of meeting the man who would change my life; not my world view, nor my goals; just my life! His emotive article 'Roebuck in the Thicket' had inspired me to respond and it thus initiated my acceleration into the mysteries, immeasurably. After an instructive but informal two year correspondence that began in 1996, Fate conspired that we should finally meet in August 1998. Acting upon guidance from whom John referred to as 'elders,' he made the immediate decision to elevate me to the position of Maid for the Clan of Tubal Cain. He became my mentor and began teaching in earnest. This initially transpired through the bulk of a manuscript he was refining as a joint venture with Chas Clifton in America following their success with *Sacred Mask, Sacred Dance*.

Wishing to present the 'Transmission' between us officially, John suggested that I compose a Foreword for this forthcoming book. Somewhat reluctantly, in my desire to remain as anonymous as possible I conceded, albeit under my then '*nom de plume*' Shani Holland-Ridge. The manuscript was completed including my own Foreword under the title: 'The Cave and the Castle' and presented to Chas Clifton for completion of his portion of the book. Due to unforeseen personal issues that emerged between them, the book was abandoned and remained unpublished and John withdrew his mss submission.

But despite the manuscript's unfortunate abandonment, some of John's work at least did realise publication when Mike Howard edited and produced *The Roebuck in the Thicket*. This was a compilation that included a selection of articles written by John for *The Cauldron* during the late 1990s. Some of this material had also featured in the abandoned collaboration with Chas Clifton. These were supplemented by the few articles of Robert Cochrane's composed and published within certain pagan/occult magazines during the final years leading up to his own tragic death in 1966. So in this fruition of labour, marked by the passing of a decade, John's previously unpublished mss, complete and unabridged, has finally achieved its long deserved publication. In keeping with John's original intention, my initial Foreword has been retained, albeit refined as the passage of time dictates. To the rest I approached the task of editing John's mss with a light hand, wishing to maintain his charm and easy style. Minor alterations only have been undertaken to improve grammar, punctuation or to remove repetitions where they occur in the original. The order of contents has been changed purely to enhance the flow of the greater narrative. Subject matter has been briefly supplemented in text and in the notation commentary by additional materials imparted by John to myself thereafter during the seven years he lived as my honoured mentor. It is thus as John intended.

Most of all, it is important to remember that John's purpose had been to disseminate the latent potential underpinning the traditions both he and Robert Cochrane had been exposed to. They do not reveal those actual traditions nor the works engaged by the Clan then or now, but retain the kernel of truth that may in turn inspire the founding of other valid operative systems. Designed for those who seek more 'traditional' methods of working, the rites discussed here present only the bare bones of genuine praxes for exploration into the mysteries. Those who choose to work rather than study them will recognize their unmistakable authenticity. Simple invocations are given where our own may not, offering again concepts embodied by them. This satisfies curiosity without compromising discretion. Here then, begins the lovingly restored and original 'Roebuck in the Thicket.'

Shani Oates, Maid of the Clan of Tubal Cain - Martinmas 2010

10

Foreword

We are 'The People of Goda, of the Clan of Tubal Cain'; a title that describes a '*people*' practising a traditional form of witchcraft, over which much speculation has been vocalized for more than four decades. Numerous debates have raised many contentious issues regarding the actions and beliefs of its founder Robert Cochrane, calling to account the veracity of the claims made for and about him. So was he really all that he asserted; or something else entirely? Such concerns become purely academic in consideration of the efficacy of all magical systems that must stand or fall on their intrinsic ability to produce requisite and genuine results. Exultation felt during ritual workings due to their inherent 'Virtue' remains the only testimony to authenticity needed. Between 'being' and 'source' a symbiosis exists that crosses the threshold of time where many have failed to rationalize and ultimately control that Virtue. No longer here to guide us through our solitary quests for knowledge, certain gifted individuals and pioneers of the esoteric occult sciences, have left us blindly groping around in the dark trying to make sense of their disparate legacies, of which so many are incomplete, fragmented or unstructured.

Evan John Jones, since the tragic death of Robert Cochrane in 1966, had kept alive the magic and spirit of one of the 20th century's most enigmatic and gifted exponents of the Craft. For over thirty years, John worked quietly, preserving a tradition known to the public as the Clan of Tubal Cain. 'Wyrd' as John would have it, then revealed to him Her plans for the continuity of the Clan. And so, deeded by an inviolate act of 'Direct Transmission,' duly documented and officially declared, it became incumbent upon me as heir to a singular role, previously held by Cochrane's widow, to hold in trust the legacy of this now historical, poetic and magical tradition as Maid of the Clan of Tubal Cain. Under this premise, the late

Magister of the Clan, E.J. Jones, requested that I fulfil my obligation to the Clan's public responsibilities in presenting this synopsis, paying particular attention to my own sense of awareness and understanding of the Clan's mysteries. Being only newly appointed as head of the Clan, I'd found this to be a daunting task. Yet it is hoped that by sharing that inspired *'joie de vivre,'* others may glean some measure of the Muse that enabled me to engage at a modest level the ancient forces at work within this vastly complex multi-verse.

Humankind has long revered the supernatural forces exuding from this colossal, omnipresent cosmos since first it grasped the ability to stand upright on the African Savannas to gaze at the arc of the starry heavens above, almost four million years ago. Humbled by this awesome perspective, our ancestors began their eternal quest for an understanding of and re-union with the elusive Primality known as the 'Source.' True 'experience' of the divine remains the prime mover amongst all magical fraternities, lodges, groups and crafters, not to mention all religions and belief systems, whether theist or deist. We are no exception to this. In fact, it is something we are ever mindful of. Moreover, due to the enigma shrouding the life, work and tragic death of the late Robert Cochrane, The Clan of Tubal Cain continues to intrigue and beguile occultists and seekers in their unfailing efforts to understand his genius, which was such that it often eluded even those closest to him. Over the last few years of his life, correspondence between Cochrane and a guest member of the Clan (a magician in his own right), the late Bill Gray, inspired two books which have since been written and successfully published.[1] The intent again, was to dispel the many bogus works claiming to be his circulating both sides of the Atlantic, in particular upon the internet, and to serve as a fitting tribute to a man who will always remain an enigmatic figure within the Craft.

Having studied the letters that sourced these two publications, I may confirm their content as heavily primed with hints and clues, inviting considered analysis of Cochrane's works. However, so dark is the veil surrounding him still that even the intimate knowledge and privileged insights of extant members of the Clan, reveal but little. Only through the actual 'Work,' can some of its magic become manifest, affording an increasing comprehension of the man behind the myth, and the myth behind the man. For those who devise rituals based upon his works, be prepared to experience something very rare – the responses are visceral and primal. Requiring no elaboration, for their Virtue lies within unsubtle simplicities and unlike many modern traditions, revived or otherwise, it bears little resemblance to paganism, remaining true to its 18th century Craft roots. But this is stated absolutely without prejudice for though they are not incompatible, they are merely intrinsically distinct. In fact, Cochrane frequently asserted that certain ideals and practices inherent within his teachings separated 'witches' from pagans. Neither blasé or ill-considered, this idiosyncratic statement is clarified as the work is studied and practised.

As the seasons unfold, the journey completes more than a celebration of the cyclical transitions between life and death; rather, the rituals concentrate more upon the focussed *will* to work in altered states rather than subscribing to an overt show of pomp and circumstance. Conversely, the work requires that we recognize our humanity in deference to our 'divinity.' It is utterly overwhelming to realise our insignificance when in the presence of that all encompassing force. Contained within the cumulative praxes of the Clan are many fundamental truths - arcane keys inspire magical consciousness buoyant within a profound cosmology. Rites that clearly echo variant forms of ancestor worship honour the Clan family, both past and present. Spatial and temporal boundaries disintegrate as the true historical legacy unfurls, transcending the notoriety of its promulgator, Robert Cochrane.

Of course no book, tome or *grammarie* nor any system of magic will provide the answer to the 'mysteries,' nor can they offer enlightenment. No, the mysteries are in themselves the pathways to gnosis – literally of 'knowing thyself,' a vital process essential before ever the real journey begins. At that point only is the prepared person 'ready' to engage in the 'Initiation' proper, with spirit on its own terms. All any teacher or mentor may provide is the environment wherein each seeker instigates their own argosy of self-discovery, nurturing and guiding them away from false-hoods and lapwings that distract the seeker from their goal. History records many such mystery Schools of which Robert Cochrane claimed to belong to 'one of the few remaining.'

Either directly or indirectly, both he and his successor Evan John Jones have been vehicles for the continuity of selective religio-historical practises reflecting concepts drawn through centuries of discreet contact. Listed among them are: Gypsy lore and medieval demonology, including influences gleaned from Sufi trance-inducing techniques. But most predominant are the threads of Anglo-Saxon lore and magic. And if we move further beyond this, we may discern traces of Indian Tantrism and even Bronze-Age animism. Of course none of these should be considered in any way as survivals, but rather as distinct yet empathic praxes periodically absorbed anew from within disparate sources of a tenacious 'Underground Stream.' It is hoped this wellspring of knowledge, accrued and so vibrantly preserved, may inspire you as much as it continues to inspire us, the 'People of Goda, of The Clan of Tubal Cain' to follow and enjoy again the glorious mysteries.

Introduction

At the core of what Robert Cochrane called 'The **Faith**'[2] resides the concept, *"Out of Chaos, the Godhead created Order."* And in creating order it also created balance, harmony, and the conditions for first creating and then sustaining life. We could say the same in different words by stating that the universe must have been preordained. Stated yet differently, it seems as though the concept of the universe relies on fundamental numbers, the electrical charge of the electron or the mass of the proton, all of which seem adjusted within critical limits, thus making possible the development of life. If the charge of the electron had been a little different, stars would not have been able to burn hydrogen, for instance. Most of the known values needed would have created an awe-inspiring universe, yet one empty of all life. An expanding universe must have a rate of expansion close to a critical rate to avoid it collapsing in upon itself. In short, out of Chaos came Order.

Humankind has always sought ways to express the concept of this 'Godhead.' Since that first glimmering of awareness, the hardest thing of all has been the coming to terms with what this all embracing totality is. The one notion that I am readily able to accept was given to us by Cochrane who likened the 'Godhead' to a multi-faceted jewel of which we could see only one face. Few are spiritually advanced enough to see more than one face of divinity, and the message they then deliver to humanity is never an easy one to live with. All too often the message is ignored or, worse, twisted and distorted to support a factional view. You have only to look at how many religions and sects claim to be the single inheritors of Divine truth, when in fact the 'truth,' like the Godhead itself, is multi-faceted. For most of us, to see one face of the Godhead can be hard enough. What most religions actively do is reduce the *reality*

15

of the Godhead to a level that most people can visualize, accept, and relate to; be it a paternal God figure or a maternal Mother Goddess. In both cases they have been molded to reflect our own family, tribal, and national experiences. After all, wasn't it said during the Victorian era that God was an English gentleman?

Cochrane expressed the ultimate Godhead in terms of a Goddess who is the Mother of Creation, yet who is also the Renewer of Life through being the Giver of Death. She manifests Herself in the warming winds of the springtime, the cooling breeze in the summer's heat and the death-dealing blasts of winter. We see Her mirrored in the seasons, for Her spirit is the very essence from which the seasons were first created. As for Her physical manifestation, we may look (as so many have done) to the Moon in all its phases. The New Moon: the Young Maiden as the virginal bride-to-be; The Full Moon: the beautiful and mature Mother, the one who still tends to the needs of all Her children. In the Waning Moon, we may see Her as the Old Hag or Crone, barren in body yet full of the wisdom that comes from the living of a full life. Thus with the Waning Moon comes the waning of earthly desires that face everyone with the onset of old age. The dark of the Moon is the 'Hidden Time' signifying death and the promise of rebirth. With the coming of the New Moon, the cycle starts again, and with its turning, new destinies are woven, new fates are cast and new lives are started.[3]

Yet it is *not* the Moon that is worshipped, but the spirit behind it. Man may have placed his footprints on the lunar surface, but the magic and mystery of the 'Goddess' as symbolized for many by the Moon, has never been touched. As long as there is one 'witch' alive to follow Her ways, they will always remain so.[4] Another tenet of our creed is how in the beginning, the Godhead seeded the Earth with tiny fragments of its own divine being, that every individual soul should each receive one spark.

16

With every successive incarnation, each soul must walk the spiral path of birth and rebirth in order to progress spiritually until it reaches a point where it is advanced enough to become reabsorbed back into the body of the Godhead. Thus in time the Godhead will be re-created from all the scattered fragments of itself, and the cycle of present existence will be fulfilled.

As I said, this is only a view that we bear in mind when we remember a primary yet basic article of the *Faith* - that of our firm belief in reincarnation. With each life, a person creates the fate or destiny that he or she will then have to live out in the next incarnation. We also believe that a soul can trap itself in the same repetitive cycle over and over again without ever moving on. Should the soul advance spiritually enough in one lifetime, it will realize this and perhaps break the pattern. There is another way for a soul to break this cycle, where someone throws it a lifeline. That happened in my case changing my personal fate, allowing me to break free of this negative pattern, paving the way for me to advance just a few more steps. Tied into this concept, Cochrane taught how there exists, not only individual souls but also 'kindred souls.' Like each separate finger upon a hand, they are joined to the others forming a mystically bonded whole.

Where Robert Cochrane and I are concerned, we met because at that time, his wife and I worked for the same company and I had offended her. As a result of this upset, he actually considered putting the 'mockers' on me. Yet for some 'reason' or another he held back. After another chance meeting with his wife, in a library of all places, I ended up being invited to their home. Supposing that he had not followed his 'gut' reaction and put the mockers on me instead, then this and all else I have written on the Craft never would have materialized. In fact, that first 'chance' encounter with them both, can only be viewed as a meeting between kindred souls reaching out to one another, a recognition in spirit of one who had lost his way, needing help back onto the path.

How many of us meet a person for the first time and feeling drawn towards them, being instantly at home in their company, as though meeting again an old friend we have not seen for many years. With some people, this bond is so finely tuned that each instinctively knows what the other is thinking, even though in temperament and upbringing they may be totally unalike. My experience here is of a re-union of kindred souls who found each other after two or three lifetimes apart. The basic premise of Cochrane's mythos is to see death as a journey that every soul must take. On one side we see the oak tree and the sacred circle with the altar-stang mounted on its edge. A path leads from the circle to the river and the ferry man. On the opposite bank, the path continues to a castle perched on a rocky outcrop. Sometimes we add the face of the Goddess slightly above and between the castle and the oak. Let's now consider the symbolic importance of each part.

The oak, as 'king of the forest' also guards the [*northern*] door to the Underworld. It was one of the seven chieftain trees named in old Irish Law; to fell any one of these unlawfully was considered a serious crime. It was to the sacred oak of *'Diana Nemorensia'* (the Roman shrine of Nemi) that any criminal could flee and escape justice, provided he survived one ordeal. Once there, he would have to fight the guardian of the shrine to the death; only then would he become the new priest and guardian. No matter how bad his crime, his role was considered sacrosanct as long as he remained within the sacred area.

Nearer to home, the Druids considered oak trees to be sacred, and their worship was held within an oak grove. In the New Forest, an area of southern England set apart as a hunting preserve by King William the Conqueror, a death occurred suggesting the sacrificial offering of a sacred king. On the afternoon of August the 2nd in 1100, his son, King William Rufus, met his death in a 'hunting accident.' He died at Lammas-tide, and if ecclesiastical reports are accurate, his body was placed on a cart, covered with a ragged cloak, and taken to Winchester, where he was quickly buried without a Christian service. One notable point stressed in particular within the account, was how his blood dripped on the ground during the cart's journey to Winchester. In fact, the whole record of his death is consistent with the myth of the divine sacrificial king dying for his people and land, of his blood fertilizing the ground where it fell. Interestingly, the place from where the fatal arrow was fired was the foot of an oak tree.[5]

The oak also guards the 'Foursquare Gateway to the Underworld.' From its boughs and hefty trunk are hewn the lintel and doorposts to the hidden realms of the Dark Lord of the Mound, and the timber coffins that encase the bleached bones of long-dead demi-gods and heroes. People gathered beneath its spreading branches to settle disputes and hear the spoken word. The most famous oak in England is of course the Great Oak in Windsor Great Park, said to be haunted by the figure of 'Herne' around Candlemas. Herne is for many, the leader of the Wild Hunt, riding the Night-Mare with the Hell Hounds at his heels, rounding up the souls of the dead.

Around England are also found a number of 'Gospel Oaks' where itinerant preachers and ranters delivered their sermons on the gospels. Often these large and solitary trees also served as boundary markers, so in a sense they stood on ground that belonged to no one. These trees became sacred and in their shade no weapon could be carried, no blow struck in anger or vengeance. Here disputes would be heard and settled, feuds settled by mutual agreement. Bargains would be struck, pacts agreed, oaths affirmed until finally, it was from under its branches that a person could be declared a 'wolf's head' and cast out of fellowship, adrift beyond the bounds of society and placed at the mercy of the gods.

It is no surprise then why so many 'witches' whenever possible, endeavour to locate a working site around or beneath an oak tree. For us, the oak is still the sacred tree, and should it draw lightning, all the better, because lightning is thought to be the sparking thunderbolt of the Old God Himself. A tree that has magic worked beneath its branches comes alive in a special way because it draws power through its roots from the very depths of the Underworld. Here it stands a silent sentinel to the portals it guards.

Next we must consider the Stang and its position in relation to the Circle and the Tree. (depicted by the graphic I + O)Placed south of the tree, on the northern edge of the circle, it becomes the icon of the Young Horn King, whom we believe reincarnates the Old Horned God, 'gathered up home again' by the Pale-Faced Goddess of the North in Her aspect as the Old Hag or Destroyer. Here the Stang marks the entrance or gateway to the working area. We translate this to signify the Young Horn King standing guard at the symbolic entrance to the Otherworld across the liminal edge of the working area, usually, though not always, a circle. He was born of the Goddess who was both lover and sister to the Old Horned God, the self-same Goddess named for Diana, forever enshrined in the sixteenth century verse quoted by T.C. Lethbridge in his book *Witches: Investigating an Ancient Religion*:

"Diana and her darling crew shall pluck your fingers fine,
And lead you forth right pleasantly to sup the honeyed wine.
To sup the honeyed wine, my loves, and breathe the heavenly air,
And dance as the young angels dance.
Ah God, that I were there."

Historically speaking,[6] any male Clan or Tribal leader was once thought of as the Sacrificial Divine God-King imbued with the essence/ Virtue of the Old God within. As the willing sacrifice killed in his prime for the good of the tribe, he would pass on that spirit of the Young God to his successor, keeping the *divine essence* strong even as the King weakened with age.

Over time, this sacrificial concept changed to such extent that a substitute was accepted where a person and then later an animal became the required sacrificial victim. Eventually, this led to the mythos of the Totem animal still commemorated by the placement of an animal mask just below the horns of the Cuveen Stang. In our case, the Totem is a ram's head. Here our animal guardian is displayed where once its actual skull might have been buried to guard the working area. Today, although the Magister is still considered as the living representative of the Young God, this office is not held in the same manner as was once understood. For with the exception of one very important ritual and one particular blessing, he is no longer considered to be the God's actual carnate form. Instead, the honour once duly given to that role is now transferred to the Stang, the modern Icon of the Old Horned God, whose presence upon the Stang preserves the potency of the once masked and horned figure of the priest and shaman propitiating the Godhead through the sacred tree.

The circle is more a 'sacred' area than a 'working' circle because it seeks to represent the area in front of the grave/mound entrance to the Underworld. At the Crickley Hill site just outside Cheltenham, a stone circle was excavated at the end of the burial mound. The site apparently began as a track-way leading to a small sanctuary or Nemeton. Later, a long barrow was built over the track way and the Nemeton was replaced by a stone circle. Although I do not claim that what we do now was ever an echo of rites held there in ancient times, we instinctively associated the circle and the grave together long before the Crickley Hill site was known.

The path from the circle to the river continues, passing between two stone pillars. A raven perches on one of them, symbolizing another hidden concept which will be explained later. [7] Next, we must consider the river. Of all symbols used to define the line between this world and the next, perhaps a river is the most enduring especially whence crossed only through death or in the death mimicry of shamanic trance. Ancient Saxon chieftains were often buried in boats, and several cultures retain still the archaic custom of placing coins on a dead person's eyes 'to pay the ferry man.'

As it crosses this liminal marker, the last vestiges of our corporeal memories are washed away from the journeying soul, saving only those core lessons learned during that lifetime. I have often wondered whether the old notion of how a witch, having shape-shifted into animal form, changes back into her own form after crossing running water, could be nothing more than a garbled form of this abstract concept. As belief in the transformation of the soul became part of an oral tradition, its real meaning gradually could have become lost. Crucial to Cochrane's tradition was his belief that the soul of a still carnate witch could cross and re-cross this river,[8] whilst that of a 'Pagan' (whom he considered to be a non-initiate) would remain with the living and limited thereafter as discarnate beings within the 'Land of the Dead.' We will return to this concept later.

Beyond the river are a waterfall and a pool. Both symbolize the gathering of knowledge. The pool reminds us of the 'Celtic' myth of the salmon that ate the nut that fell from the magical hazel tree; thus whoever ate the salmon gained wisdom. Robert Cochrane always equated wisdom with knowledge gained through divination, and one of the old ways of discovering the future was through the ritual of *'Jaghairm.'* This involved the diviner wrapping himself in the hide of a freshly killed ox. After the needful questions had been put to him, he was left as close to a waterfall as possible, where he stayed until he had the answer. No doubt the hypnotic sound of falling water helped erase his awareness of the physical world. Foregoing the rather doubtful pleasures of the still warm hide, I am able to vouch for the efficacy of this method, having achieved remarkable results on a hunting trip, long ago.

The waterfall also reminds us that there is another form of Craft working rather the usual celebratory ones involving aspects drawn from shamanic traditions. Such practices exampled by the *'Jaghairm Rite'* guide us to seek out wisdom and knowledge from *beyond the grave* itself. Having crossed the river, one faces the wastelands, the place of desolation and dust. In the Arthurian tradition, this was the spellbound land where the Cauldron/Grail keeper lays crippled waiting for a 'seeker of truth' who will answer the key question:

"Whom does the Grail serve?"

If the question can be correctly answered, then the keeper recovers and the wastelands will bloom again. Here the old stories transform the essence of 'Celtic' birth, death, and rebirth myth cycle including the riddling traditions, which in turn were blended with Christian myths of the Holy Grail to form the Arthurian Myth Cycle. Both contain the idea of a magical transformation of the barren wastelands. But in our tradition, this is achieved through the ritual of the 'Rose beyond the Grave,' which in turn forms part of the death and resurrection cycle central to the 'Old Faith.'

On a rocky outcrop beyond the wasteland stands 'The Castle that spins without motion between Two Worlds.' Here we re-enter a world [*similar to that preserved*] in Celtic legend, where the dying king is carried (usually crossing over water) to return at some future date to aid his people in a time of great need. Of neither Heaven nor this Earth, the 'Castle' of the Clan is reached only by crossing water. It has the ability to 'disappear and reappear at will,' meaning that it will manifest itself only to the chosen few and under certain very specific conditions. The original Castle was created by visionary mystics and Bardic poets trying to give form to what is, after all, an abstract spiritual dimension. Being poets and mystics, they were dream-weaving the Castle as a concept in such a way as to maintain its magico-mystery elements.

To seek this elusive Castle, with its dark-stained turrets, there is no better place to begin than from a cliff top looking outwards, over the sea at sunset, where you may gaze upon the ever-changing cloud formations on the horizon. Watching the clouds can induce a mild trance where the imagination roams free, and it will be then that you may glimpse the Castle, [*on the liminal rim suspended aloft twixt sea and sky*] the edge of its dark towers stained red by the setting Sun, with its misty black base suspended below. If you have a poet's soul, you will begin to understand something of the Castle's enchantment; and as its shape changes slowly with the clouds, you begin to understand what is sometimes meant by '*spinning without motion between two worlds.*' Logically, you have seen a trick of the light; yet deep down, you are left with the impression that you have seen something 'beyond' this world. You have glimpsed Her Enchanted Castle that the questing soul journeys to, shifting in:

"... the golden sunset, my love. Into the golden rest."

It is important to realise that so potent an image as the Castle cannot be relegated to nor contained by the twilight world of Celtic myths but is established within many uniquely British traditions through its qualities sympathetic to the Matter of Britain, exampled within the Arthurian

Cycle and Grail Romances. As new attributes were added to the core concepts of the Castle, they enhanced its mythopoetic appeal.

Our tradition describes the 'Castle' as the 'dwelling-place' of the Pale-Faced Goddess, dropping completely the idea of questions supposedly asked by the guardian of the gateway (the Nameless Knight). These usually took the form of 'Whom does the Cauldron serve?' or 'Who makes the wasteland bloom?' And bloom it does, with green shoots and winding tendrils that blossom into blood-red roses, transforming what was barren into a lush landscape. If the initiate knew the answers, it proved they had the requisite 'gnosis,' and he or she was assured of entry to the Castle and consequent immortality. However, since we believe in reincarnation, we hold that the soul journeys to this Castle to await rebirth. At the same time, the 'Cauldron' is regarded as the Vessel of Inspiration, traditionally guarded by nine maidens [sometimes seven].

It may seem strange to couple birth and death with knowledge, wisdom, and inspiration. Yet in light of a belief in reincarnation it all makes sense. Without death, there can be no life. Without life, there cannot be any of its emotions: love, hate, harshness, and compassion. Neither could the evils humanity inflicts upon itself exist, nor the greatness of spirit that can lift us above them. Not only does the Cauldron restore life to the dead through rebirth, it also generates new ideas, new thinking, art, poetry, and music - in short, all the things that separate us from our primitive ancestors whose souls, if the theory of reincarnation is right, must inhabit some of the bodies of today.

Returning to the three slowly revolving towers of the Castle, a nebulous image of the Goddess hovers above them. Although She seems to be at the apex of the concept, behind Her is yet another aspect of the Godhead, a mystery. Her face is but one facet of the formless, ageless, and infinitely remote source of all living things which we call the Spirit of Creation. Because it is difficult to come to terms with the concept of pure spirit, we humanize it, giving it form and shape, and place it between us and the Divine Intelligence that first laid down the numerical value of the charge of the electron which allowed the universe to develop in the way it has, thus generating all life. By this point, some people may be saying:

> "Hold on a minute, this isn't anything like the Craft I know. So if this is right, where does it leave me? Is everything that I've been doing wrong?"

The answer to that is no. In a letter to the late ceremonial magician William G. Gray (who before his death passed his collection of letters from Robert Cochrane over to me), Cochrane raised this very point, and I can do no better than to quote his actual words:

> "When I am dead, I shall go to another place that myself and my ancestors created. Without their work it would not exist, since in my opinion, for many eons of time the human spirit had no abode, then by desire to survive created the pathway into other worlds. Nothing is got by doing nothing, and whatever we do now creates the world in which we exist tomorrow. The same applies to death; what we have created in thought, we create in that other reality. Desire, as you probably know better than I, was the very first of all created things."[9]

So by being somewhat assertive about our world view and that of our eventual fate after death, we have the opportunity while in this world to help create then maintain our own little niche in that other reality. Whatever sort of heaven or paradise we want, we can thus generate it, providing of course we both desire and believe in it unmitigatedly. Conversely, if we believe in nothing, then 'nothing' is what we will get after death. To this end, specific symbols and rituals help to reinforce our beliefs and maintain the continuity of our particular tradition, which will preserve that Otherworld place where our souls take respite while awaiting rebirth. Everything written beyond this point is our way of seeing and doing things. If it helps others to clarify their own ideas of what they want from 'The *Faith*,' or if they wish to interweave some of this material with their own, let them feel free to do so. It worked for Cochrane, it worked for me, and it should work equally well for you.

Evan John Jones, Brighton, Sussex

To E. John Jones

"Ðæt wæs god cyning!"

The Wanderer

Always alone, the solitary one awaits the herald,

Fate's favour, though sorrowful of heart,

Through the water-way, Long

Stirred by hand, along Ice-cold sea

5   Goes the path of the exile. Fate is wholly inexorable!

Thus spoke the Wanderer, Mindful of hardship,

Grievous murderer, dear kinsmen's downfall:

'Oft I must, Before each dawn,

Make sorrowful lament. None now live

10   To whom my heart's Remembrances dare

Openly tell. I truth do know

That it is among the rune-masters A noble custom,

That he his spirit-chest fasten fast,

Guard his heart, consider such his Desires.

15   None of weary heart can Fate resist,

Nor he, troubled of heart, can help bring to pass.

Therefore the righteous, often sorrowful

Within his heart, binds it fast;

So my spirit I shield.

20 Oft saddened, of home bereft,

Kinsmen far distant, Fettered and bound,

Since long of old my kindly lord

Earth's darkness conceals, and I humble thence

Impassioned by many winters over waves binding,

25 Sought the Hall-Sorrowful, Bestowed of treasure,

Where I, far or near, Might chance to find

The one in the mead-hall that knew me,

Or me friendless would console,

Accustom with delights. Wise men know

30 How cruel is sorrow as a gift

To him who has few beloved protectors:

The path of an exile claims him, not twisted gold,

Heart frozen, not earthly glory.

Remembers he hall-men and receiving the gift of his Lord,

35 How in youth his generous Lord

Accustomed him to feasting. Joys all fallen!

Therefore know the man whose beloved lord's

Dear counsel long forwent:

Then sorrow and sleep combine together, the

40 Wretched solitary one is oft bound,

His thoughts in spirit that he his lord

Embraced and kissed, and on knee laid

Hand and head, thus he sometimes

In days gone by enjoyed the throne.

45   Then awaken again friendless man,

Vision before him a dark wave,

Bathing seabirds, spread feathers,

Fall frost and snow, hail mingled.

Then be that heavy heart wound,

50   Sorely afterwards beloved. Sorrow is restored.

Then the spirit of kin pervades the mind,

Greets joyfully, eagerly examines every part

Man's companion; swim often away.

The seabird spirit vision brings many

55   Familiar utterance. Care be renewed

As he must send frequently

over wave his binding weary heart.

Therefore I cannot think through this world

For why my heart does not grow dark

60   Then I the nobleman's life meditated upon.

How he suddenly left the hall

Brave young retainer. So this middle earth

Each day declines and falls;

For none can be a wise man, before he has

65   Wintered in the Kingdom of the world. Wise men must wait,

None must be too impulsive, nor be too hasty of speech,

Nor be too weak a warrior, nor too reckless,

Nor too afraid, nor too rejoicing, nor too greedy,

Nor never proud, too eager, before he readily know.

70   Man must await, when he utters vows,

Or stout-hearted know clearly

Whither heart's thoughts will turn.

The wise man understands how spectral it will be,

When all the world's estate stands deserted,

75   As now so manifold throughout this middle earth

Wind blown walls stand,

Frost covered snow-swept buildings.

Then halls decay, their lords lie

Dream deprived, heavenly host fallen

80   Proud by the walls. Some wars take away,

Carried forth, one man the bird lifted

Over high sea, another the hoary wolf

Death shared, one sad-faced man

In cave a nobleman concealed.

85 Similarly, the Creator laid waste this city of men,

As far as the inhabitants' faithless revelry,

Ancient giant workmanship stands in vain.

He who on this foundation wisely thinks

And this dark life deeply meditates,

90 Wise in spirit, far oft he remembers

Battle numbers, and these words utter:

'Where now the horse?

Where now the youth?

 Where now the ring-giver?'

Where now the throne? Where the hall revelry?

Oh bright cup! Oh mailed warrior!

95 Oh glorious Lord! How that time has passed,

Dark under night's helm, though they'd not been.

Stand now behind beloved host

Wall wondrous high, serpents gleaming.

Nobleman spirited away by the power of the Ash-tree,

100 Spear greedy for death, the glory of wyrd,

And this storm dashed cliff,

Snowstorms fall and bind the earth,

Winter's tumult, then blackness comes,

Grows dark the shadow of night, the North sends forth

105 Troubling hailstorm against the hero.

All is fraught with hardship in this earthly kingdom,

Changing fate creates the world under Heaven.

Here be money temporary, here be friends temporary,

Here be man temporary, here be woman temporary,

110 All this earthly foundation becomes in vain!'

So spoke the wise spirit, sat apart in the mysteries.

Good is he who truth preserves

nor must he grieve too quickly

The man that his heart has known, unless he already

The remedy knows

The hero with courage must act. Well is he who angels seek,

115 Solace within the Father in Heaven, where for us all He fast stands.

(Translated from the original by Ian Chambers)

1
The
Old
Covenant

"The Old Covenant binds its people with a kinship bestowed by divine grace through time, beyond manifest form as a cohesive unit for its survival and continuity rather than its dissemination and diaspora." (Levy)

Although rarely mentioned or even highlighted within much of the modern literature written about the Craft, Traditional Witchcraft remains built upon a *pact between* us and the 'Old Ones.'[10] Still, this relationship is vital and it contributes to the group life of the Cuveen. This particular ritual should only be performed when necessity dictates, for the 'Covenant' that it expresses should hold for the duration of the working relationship between the Cuveen's Magister and Maid. In fact, I have witnessed it **twice only**. This is as it should be for the active term of the Maid and Magister, which should endure for many years. It is a complex ritual, because it communicates one of the core mysteries of the Craft: the relationship between the Cult of the Dead and the Cult of Fertility and the Virtue that binds them as one.

When the Craft in its various forms began to appear in public in the mid-twentieth century, it was common to hear witches describe themselves as followers of an 'ancient fertility religion.' Since the Earth is quite obviously not short on human beings these days, 'fertility' was usually defined in the sense of personal creativity or as fertility for an overstressed/ under resourced planet. Some of us, after all, may continue to think that good crops, fertile livestock, and good hunting have their place in the cosmic scheme. But however 'fertility' is defined, we persist in our thinking that these are gifts from the gods made manifest through the rituals and magic of the priesthood. As Robert Cochrane put it:

> "the ritual of the Old Covenant[11] speaks of the time of the rutting deer, the circle of the dead when the Hunter, Old Tubal Cain and the Roebuck in the Thicket are one and the same thing-, the Divine Presence. The time when the ancient God of the mysteries, who by tradition passed on his powers through himself and into the female worshiper (expressed by) the time when the Sun King and the Moon Queen mated underground in the deepest of silence."

Diverse cultures relate this concept when the gods loved the mortals and passed on some of their divinity to them in the act of love, in many ways. Today the 'Old Ones' no longer manifest themselves to humanity in the same way that these traditions inform us; instead, the power [Virtue] that is the *Old Covenant* can only be passed on through love between a man and a woman. Only in love can it be used, because love in all forms is one and the same force: the *will* of divinity; the mark of the gods on humankind. During this sacred act, 'The Virtue of the Four Airts' are transmitted from the old Magister to the new Maid. In turn, one year's hence, she will deed these to her chosen Magister as successor to the old Magister. These Airts are possibly known to some; their usage by the Magister remains determined by discretion or necessity.

We strive to ratify the 'Rite' of the Old Covenant at the dark of the Moon as near to All Hallow's Eve as possible, and should the actual Void of the Moon fall on All Hallow's Eve itself, then any normal working would be abandoned in favour of it. Midnight is often regarded as the witching hour, and upon this night, this is doubly so. It is the night when the Mound opens for the Wild Hunt, led by a [local horned psychopomp, such as] Herne[12] to ride across hill and dale, retrieving all lost souls, gathering them up within the ancestral train to take them: *"back home again."*

Folklore relates this as the night when various spectral hearses driven by 'the Devil' race through the night with his hell hounds following in a pack behind. Whatever myth is believed, magic certainly permeates the air on All Hallow's Eve distinguishing it from all others. So it is little wonder that traditional witches continue to hold it in high regard, choosing this particular night for a very special ceremony. In fact, it is why we commemorate the 'gathering in' by the Egregore of all its souls, held and mediated through an initial and fateful transmission. Each year thereafter, it is celebrated as the 'Covenant of Hallows.'

While some parts of the rite of the 'Old Covenant' are specific to our tradition so will not be given here, a broad outline is presented, and any interested group may create their own form of the 'Covenant' based upon it. As written, the rite contains a sexual element (as do most Craft rituals, even if only symbolically), and it is the only rite of the Clan of Tubal Cain where sex between Magister and Maid is mandatory for a specific ritual reason. In fact, the lineage is thus perpetuated between a single working pair, from one generation to their next successors, from Maid to Magister to Maid and so on for the whole Clan of Tubal Cain.

In my case, when the *last* Lady of the Clan laid down her Office, before she did so, she deeded the Clan spirit into my keeping in the hope that I would be able to keep it alive. After very many years, I have finally found someone who is suitable to hold the Office of the Lady/Maid of the Clan of Tubal Cain. To her, I will pass over the Stang, sickle, cup and knife and with it, the spirit of the Clan into her care knowing full well that they will be in safe hands. Until now, there has been no-one to whom I could entrust this sacred office.

Finally, in this act I may discharge my duty to the Old Ones [13]

" ...Cochrane ...claimed the head of the Clan must always be male. This was because it symbolized the occult truth that the physical world is the mirror image of the spiritual world. What we call reality in this world must be the opposite of the inner one. Accordingly, Cochrane assigned the inner or spiritual world to the Goddess, while retaining the physical one to the stewardship of the Master...all Magisters, past, present and future both took and held their power from the Maid, who was recognized...as the living representative of the Goddess in the physical world. That is why, even today...the Clan may only offer to the Master, duty under the Law. To the Maid, they offer total loyalty, devotion and obedience, which surely ranks higher than any duty owed to the Master...[and why he stands as head] because the Maid granted him the power to do so through the 'First Rite'."[14]

Preparation:

Lay the compass with a fire in its centre. Place a pot or cauldron on the fire and fill it with a 50-50 mixture of wine and water. Place the Clan Stang in the north, with crossed arrows but un-garlanded outside the 'circle' or working area allotted for this rite. Instead, lay a sickle against the foot of the Stang, blade uppermost. Here the Stang again symbolizes the Virtue of the Old Horned God, visualized as a cloaked and hooded figure with a naked broadsword between his hands, pointing downwards. He is the dark warrior figure and King of the Underworld, the fearsome guardian of the Mound and wild rider of the hunt. Death is the gift he brings to himself.

The crossed arrows on the Stang represent the four cardinal points +, also denoting the equal-armed cross of the four elements **x** (earth; air; fire; water). These arrows specifically remind us that [the Goddess aspected as] Diana, the divine huntress, may shoot Her devotees with them. Such persons, Her victims will then spend the rest of their lives enamoured by Her singular beauty, seeking Her out with aching heart and restless spirit on moonlit nights. Likewise, the sickle's upward-pointing blade reminds us of She who will: *"gather us up home again."*

Just as the grain is harvested when it is ripe, so are we. When our time is done, we too are cut down. Yet as the seed falls from the harvested grain, there is promise of new life through its regeneration within fertile ground. Though given as an analogy, the seeds of grain equate well with the spiritual seed of the Old Horned God; fertility here is indeed not of this world. Unlike most Clan rituals, much of the *'Rite of the Old Covenant'* takes place beyond the periphery of the inner ritual circle, although still within the overall sacred working area normally ascribed to the Clan. We do not regard this small 'circle' as a magical circle in quite the same way as Wiccans may for example, nor is it quite the same as the ceremonial circle which both require consecration. Rather, we regard it as a sacred area- a Nemeton, in fact. This is a temple in which people are free to move in and out off, as the ritual dictates. The circle is only formally enclosed for the final stages of the rite, where it then becomes a true magical circle.

Purification:

Before going further, one must first make their peace with the gods. How this is done remains the prerogative of the individual. But, if desired, one may choose to make a confession of Faith to the Old gods through the Magister. Having done so, all participants then assemble around the Stang/altar at the northern gateway, facing the circle. The Magister stands with the Stang at his back, facing the gathering (outwards). Called the 'Devil,' by some, it is important to understand that he is not, nor could ever be the Christian Satan, but the Old Horned God's living representative on Earth. In this guise, those present may repeat their oath to 'Him,' adjured upon admittance to the Clan. Having accepted his due as Old Hornie's representative, he must then pronounce a blessing upon the gathering. Finally, all present must bow before 'Him' three times: one each for the Stang; the crossed arrows, and the sickle.

Charging the Pot:

Turning back into the circle, the Magister uses a whetstone to perform a token sharpening of the knife he is carrying. Plunging the knife briefly into the pot, it is removed and he then paces the ring widdershins (counter-clockwise). The pot or cauldron is charged by this ritual knife and with the full focussed intention by the group. He repeats the action two more times. The rest of the group may chant or remain silent. He then stands aside by the Stang with his back to the people (facing inwards) waiting behind him, to come in.

Next to enter is a woman of the Cuveen who represents the *'Pale-Faced Goddess.'* She stands silently by the fire waiting. Three women enter next, holding aloft a tray upon which are three bound bundles of herbs: a sweet one to represent the joys of life, a bitter one for the sorrows of life, and a third one, the herb of grace. They elevate the tray to the heavens in silence together and then take it slowly over to the pot, where each of them place one bundle. As they do so, the 'Pale Lady/Madame la Guiden' announces their identification and purpose. They all retire to the northern point of the circle. Robert Cochrane summed up the symbolism of the triple offering when he explained it this way:

"Witchcraft is something like gardening, something like cooking; it is a little bit of everything starting off with the basic ingredients. We are the stew or potage in the cauldron, the roots, the trunk, the leaves and the tree. It is dependent on ourselves how we flourish or wither with the winter's storm."

Thus when the 'Pale Lady' first binds the triple offering before it is taken to the Cauldron, her actions state that we each as individuals bring something of our own individuality to the melting pot there to blend with the gifts that others in the group themselves have brought. As the children of Goda of the Clan of Tubal Cain we realize the Cauldron of Inspiration offers gifts from the Goddess Herself. We acknowledge that each herb represents a level of existence upon *Her Tree*: with the cup taken from the pot, we share this awareness with each other and with Her. Remember, we may only take from the Cauldron what we each put in.

Hallowing the Quarter/Cardinal points:

Four men (ideally) enter next. One carries the sword given to him by the Magister. They should space themselves around the cauldron. He that wields the sword should plunge its point into the pot, while the three remaining men touch his sword arm at the hand or wrist with their right hands for a few seconds. Stepping back, they can begin to circle the cauldron and the fire deosil (clockwise) until each person reaches his assigned quarter post. The man holding the sword should be stationed in the North. He must then plunge the sword into the pot again. This is lifted out and turning outwards, he must flick it sharply towards his station.

The sword is then passed clockwise to the next man [in the East] who repeats his action, and so on until the sword reaches North again. The Magister is then handed back his sword. Taking it to the gateway, he forms the bridge by crossing the sword and besom together [X] bisecting the edge of the 'ring'. Everyone including himself departs, crossing the bridge. In the present, our group had grown accustomed to performing this part of the ritual in silence; however, that is not a strict rule. So if any group following this rite feel they have a need for words to mark the Hallowing of the Quarters, there is absolutely no reason for them not to.

The lady soon to be elevated as Maid of the Covenant should then enter the ring along with the Magister, who carries with him the cup and the ladle. He presents the ladle to the Maid, who dances three times widdershins around the pot and fire whirling it around her head. Filling the cup from the cauldron, she empties it upon the ground as a libation while evoking the combined forces of the Sun King and Moon Queen. She then announces to the gathering a directive to join them in the act of worship.[15] All cuveeners re-enter, crossing the bridge. She must then refill the cup held by the Magister; handing him the ladle, she takes the cup and beginning with the Magister, she offers each member a sip from the cup:

"We drink this wine in our Lady's name as a symbol and a reminder of the bounty from Her cauldron."

When everyone has taken a sip and any remaining wine has been tipped onto the ground, the Summoner stands facing the South with his back to the fire. With a backward kick of his left foot, he overturns the cauldron so that what is left of the wine and water spills over the fire and splashes to the North. His action creates a final libation poured to the Goddess in Her aspect as Earth Mother to whose womb the mortal remains of all living things must one day return.

Everyone may now line up to prepare for the Mill with the Magister following along hindmost, lifting and wielding the Stang he brings it into the centre of the working space. Contrary to usual practice, we mark the bridge at this point, leaving it undisturbed, signifying that the ritual is devotional rather than magical. All participants pace the Mill until brought to an instinctive halt. The Summoner will then lead everyone out (except the Maid and Magister who remain) across the bridge to a separate place within the enclosure, warmed by another fire, which has been tended by a member of the 'Watch.'

After a few moments of meditative silence, the Magister calls on the Sun King and Moon Queen to descend upon him and the Maid with words such as these exampled here:

> "By the will of divinity, the mark of the gods upon man, be thou with us in body, soul and spirit, so that in our mating within the sacred darkness, we become vessels conjoined through love of thee, affirming the ancient Covenant of our ancestors, invoked this day before the stars who bear witness to this timeless act."

This invocation is repeated three times, and each time it is said, the end of the Stang is thumped on the ground. After a few moments of silence, the Magister replaces the Stang setting it up again, replacing the sickle at its foot. Bowing silently three times before the Stang, he then withdraws the bridge, separating the space from the cuveeners beyond it, before returning to the central fire. Now the ring is deemed 'closed' and charged as the sacred inner sanctum of the Nemeton.

The Magister and the Maid prepare themselves for the 'Sun and Moon Rite,' performed by tradition to consummate in Sacred Marriage, the Old Covenant in silence and in darkness.[16] Upon completion of this most holy act, they re-light the cardinal lamps, and build the bridge (Gyfu) across the threshold as a signal to the Summoner to lead the gathering back in to their 'circle.' The Magister takes the newly elevated Maid[17] by the hand, leading her to the altar/ Stang. He turns her around to face the gathering, having formed a semi-circle in front of her. Thereafter, the Magister is no longer looked upon as the Divil of the Clan, a fact he

42

announces as he unveils the Maid, presenting her to the gathering with these words:

Magister: "Behold thy Maid, who will serve our Cuveen well."

The Cuveen will then offer the Maid a white (soul) candle and a kiss of homage, each member in turn as a token of their acceptance of her as the Maid of their Clan. The 'Rite of the Old Covenant' is only for the willing. No Maid may be forced into it. On the contrary, it is up to her to claim from the Magister her right to enter into the Old Covenant, her sacred marriage with the Magister, evoking his ancient dual role as priest-king of the Cuveen and the living representative of the Old Horned God on Earth. When the cuveeners offer their homage, it is to these deities, *not* to the individuals who represent them. The white candles that they lay at her feet stand for the care of their souls, for the candle evokes the 'soul candle' lit during Full Admission into the Clan.

By thus offering it to the Maid in this way, one is pledging oneself in a manner that goes far beyond the more general spoken oath, now given in gesture here to a person rather than the group. Although no actual oath-taking forms part of this ceremony, it is assumed the participants already know and accept what is implied and what they are called upon to offer. Finally, the Maid may yet demand that every *new* member thereafter similarly offer her their soul candle, laying it at her feet, to make a personal oath to and through her to the Moon Queen, Goddess of the Night.

2
The
Roebuck
in the
Thicket

In a letter to the late William G. Gray concerning the Old Covenant, Cochrane mentions somewhat enigmatically: *"the roebuck in the thicket."* Many of us in the Clan and related traditions have been guilty of going on about the 'roebuck' without defining our terms. So what do we mean by: *"the roebuck in the thicket."*

First of all, this concept is far older and larger than the modern Craft. Many ancient cultures hold certain stories sacred that relate the entanglement within wild shrubbery, of a horned or antlered animal. The best-known of these is the puzzling tale of the biblical patriarch Abraham, ordered by his tutelary deity to sacrifice his son Isaac. (Genesis 22) Yahweh commands Abraham, as a test of his obedience, to take his beloved son into the land of Moriah, to build an altar, stack it with firewood, and sacrifice the boy child. As Abraham raised his knife an angel intervened, steadied his hand and informed him that the beast of sacrifice is elsewhere. Abraham looked around to see a ram trapped by its horns in a thicket and duly sacrificed that unfortunate animal instead. This Hebrew version of the story emphasizes obedience, so that when Yahweh sees that Abraham would even willingly sacrifice his son, He praised him, promising that his descendents will be as numerous:

"as the stars in the sky and the grains of sand on the seashore."

The Craft, by contrast, does not emphasize unquestioning obedience and our understanding of this important symbolic picture differs from the above version given in Genesis. Although we still understand the myth as being relative to sacrifice, it is in the willing self-sacrifice in *leadership*. We believe that the Antlered God was revered during the Palaeolithic era when hunting provided important food and skins for clothing. Early people dependent upon wild herds of deer, were known to have used sympathetic magic to aid their hunters and to keep the herds fertile.

Famous cave paintings and other anthropological evidence suggest that the shaman danced, clothed as a deer in deep trance to commune with the spirit of the hunt, much as the indigenous tribes of America once did, performing a magical dance that mimicked the hunt and the kill. Even today, some big-game hunters in the Craft continue to perform variations on this ancient rite. In time the image of the man dressed as a deer and the Stag/God of the herds became blurred. When the herds were eventually domesticated and farming gained importance, this blurring simplified rather than complicated the perceived image of the Horned God, now a more generalized symbol of fertility, especially within modern paganism.

Under Christianity, when the country was divided into the estates of feudal lords and all hunting and fishing rights were owned by them, the peasantry still looked to the forest for food, especially during harsh winters, hence the number of draconian game laws needed to protect the noble deer. As for the Horned God, he was slowly evolving as a template for the adversary of Christ. The aristocracy had deposed him as Lord of the Forest and its creatures. The Magister of the Clan parallels the Stag as leader, in fact he is its mystical leader, and in the past he might easily have been looked upon as the living representative of the Horned

45

God, a role he continues to enact in ritual. Bear in mind that many early religious concepts were based on what people saw reflected within their world view, typically within the world of plants and animals. Thus, even as the leadership of a herd might pass from one animal to another, so even the Horned God could be *reincarnated into one leader and then magically transferred to another.*

As the anthropologist Sir James Frazer hypothesised in *The Golden Bough*, the duration of the term of office for any priest/king of an earlier civilization could have been entirely dependent upon their strength and virility. That being so, we could say that the spirit of the Horned God diminished as the priest/king aged, hence the recurring concept in myth of the seven-year reign. On his seventh year of office, this priest/leader, or as he was known to both the Anglo-Saxons and the Norse, the *'godi,'* would offer up a blood sacrifice for another seven years of office, leading to an obvious question: What did he sacrifice? One clue comes from the book *English Society in the Early Middle Ages* by Lady Doris Stenton.

The author mentions an event that happened in Rockingham forest in 1255. After a day's hunting in the woods, a group of thirteen hunters killed a fine stag. Cutting off its head, they mounted it onto a static pole in the middle of a clearing, with the deer's mouth open, facing the rising Sun. In its open jaw they had placed a spindle, a noteworthy point missed by Lady Stenton. This was no doubt due to her lack of familiarity with the Old Craft. She perceived this ritual as a crude but light-hearted way of denigrating King Henry III, who was at odds with much of the aristocracy. In spite of this, she recorded it as the offering of: *'the Roebuck in the Thicket.'*

Several factors point to that conclusion. First of all, the thirteen hunters equate with a significant number within occultism, especially of the alleged complement of a working coven. That this number was stressed is no coincidence. The fact that the beast was decapitated after the kill and its head mounted on a pole provides another vital clue. Mounting the stag's head in this way suggests to me the hunters were making an altar or Stang, and one dedicated to the old Horned God. The severed head of the once-living deer would have made an appropriate offering to the Horned God in his domain, the wooded glade. Finally, in placing the stag's head towards the Sun, we have a double emphasis upon the solar symbol, quintessential to the 'Masculine mysteries'. This is further confirmed in the hunt itself, together with the elements of sacrifice, making the whole gesture a symbolic offering to the Male God himself.

Perhaps the most telling clue of all, albeit the smallest and most enigmatic, is the spindle the hunters placed within the jaws of the stag. The spindle speaks to us of Wyrd, of human lives as threads spun then woven into the fabric of their fate before they are cut at the allotted time. Mythically then, we could say that this stag from its moment of birth was fated to die at the hands of these thirteen hunters as the sacrifice of the seven-year priest/leader. Likewise, the hunter was fated (as he saw it) to meet the stag at this particular point in time and kill it in exchange for seven more years of office.

Hard as it may be for us to accept, the Anglo-Saxons believed in a pre-determined fate that governed the destiny of every living being. So even if the hunt leader had known he would be killed instead of the stag, he would have still gone on the hunt because his Wyrd as '*god*' of the Clan so dictated. The Horned God in the shape of the stag would then claim his soul, leaving his place to be filled by another. To those of us who were part of Cochrane's old group, the role of Wyrd within the concept of '*Roebuck in the Thicket*' is central to the Clan's mythos.

In another letter to William Gray, Cochrane laid bare many of our core beliefs of the Clan of Tubal Cain to him, stating that we are the

People of the Priest/leader of the Clan of Tubal Cain, linked to a distinctly Anglo-Saxon root tradition. He claimed to be:

> "a Pellar and a member of the people of Goda, of the Clan of Tubal Cain."

Cochrane also wrote:

> "The hunter and the hunted (old Tubal Cain) and the Roebuck in the Thicket, are one and the same thing - Divine Presence. This is the time of the God of mysteries."

Taken on a superficial level, this statement seems to not make sense. Tubal Cain is the smith-God of the forge. *So why should a smith-God become as one with the hunted?* Why should he be part of the hunting mythos described in the 'Roebuck in the Thicket'? It seems out of character for Tubal Cain to be thus involved. But if we look deeper into this mystery, then the sacrificial descent down from the Horned God, through the Priest/King into his totemic symbol of office upon his Staff/Stang, clearly reveals that at some mythical level the concept of sacrifice and Kingship bound them together.

So was this blending accidental or deliberate? We are not sure, but however this occurred, outside the Clan it was not something commonly known in the early decades following the war, especially at the time of Cochrane's correspondence with William Gray.[18] Possibly, in our distant Anglo-Saxon past, an influential synthesis occurred that enriched the strands of complementary mysticisms feeding into it. This could easily have evolved into the current version of the Tubal Cain mythos. I am not claiming this did happen this way, but it could have. Certainly there is much within our mythos that would support this theory.

Many stories of the God Woden, whose name is commemorated in place names over much of England, such as Wansdyke (Woden's dike) in the Vale of Puwsey; Wornshill near Sittingbourne, and Wodnesborough near Sandwich express the far-reaching influence of this dark-age deity. You will find Woden-linked place names scattered throughout Essex, Kent, Sussex, and as far afield as Somerset, Staffordshire, and Derbyshire amongst other places.

Treat the following passage as a 'guided visualization' after reading it through at least once. It may help you to get a feel for the ways of the people who revered this deity.

"If, in the past, you found yourself walking along one of the ancient hilltop track-ways, and if you paused at a junction where two paths crossed, and if there was a gallows with a hanging man upon it, you would pause to ponder a while. You would look at the grisly corpse, and you might notice two ravens that had flown up from the foot of the structure and perched on its crossbar, gazing down at you with dark, unblinking eyes. Having stopped for a moment, you move on. Then from out of the hilltops' early-morning mist, you see a tall cloaked hooded figure coming towards you, using a massive broad-bladed spear as a walking staff. Being more than a little frightened, you step off the track to let him pass, and as he does so, you notice that not only is he bearded but he is also one-eyed. Silently he passes you; then you too move on, only to stop after a few yards and turn to see what this ominous stranger was doing. If he stands at the foot of the gallows staring up at the dangling corpse with intense interest, then you know you have seen the old God Woden walking this Earth again and once more claiming his own."

Why would Woden stand at the gibbet's foot staring up at the hanging body with such interest? The Anglo-Saxons knew him as the Divine Magician who through self-immolation, brought wisdom to mankind. Thus he was God both of *death and of knowledge*. Both the early English and the Norse sacrificed captives by hanging, which made them sacred to Woden. So when Woden stands at the gallows' foot, he recognizes his own wherein both he and the hanged man share a common fate. The *hunter and the hunted are here one and the same*, embodied within the swinging corpse of the hanging man.

Other traditions regarding hanged felons and captives may similarly relate to this legend of Woden. For example, the severed hand of a hanged man could be transformed by appropriate magical rites into the 'Hand of Glory,' which, mounted on an altar with the fingers serving as candles, was once used in the pursuit of High Magic. The children's game of knucklebones stems from an old tradition of using the finger bones of a hanged man to foretell the future, all of which leads us back to the connection between the hanged sacrificial victim, death, magic, and wisdom.

Granted, another equally old tradition holds that crossroads in ancient Greece and Rome were sacred to Diana of the Three Ways: '*Diana Trivium*,' and also to the non-Olympian Goddess of Magic: Hekate, both of whom later became known as witch divinities. Within the Clan of Tubal Cain, the 'People' believe that our ancestors, whether Pagan or Christian, would have been more familiar and conversant with Woden. Folk memory tends to blur dates and places, but it frequently retains the general outline of the story, that little grain of a mythos that remains true to its roots.

The Christian missionaries who converted the Saxon kingdoms in the seventh century forced Woden into a limbo of the Old gods, but he was not entirely forgotten, as his appearance in the 'Lay of the Nine Herbs' reveals.[19] So is it really stretching the imagination too much to see that when a gallows was placed at a crossroads it activated the folk memory of a place once reserved for sacrificing prisoners of war to the Old gods by hanging them? Likewise, Woden's patronage of magic, prophecy and poetry blended effortlessly with the arts and smith-magic of Tubal Cain until, in Robert Cochrane's practice, they became 'as one' within his Clan of Tubal Cain. Accept this, and you can see why we called ourselves the 'cloaked/hooded witches'[20] and preferred to meet out of doors under a hilltop oak or where two tracks met and crossed, rather than hold elaborate indoor ceremonies.

Cochrane may have been working to a tradition handed down to him from the past, or perhaps it was something that he stumbled on finding an old, overgrown, but recognizable path in the Otherworld and following it to his final fate. Either way, it worked. Who knows? But what manifested itself at many of our meetings might not have simply been Tubal Cain, but also the spirit of 'Od' of old Woden himself, brought back from the realms of outer darkness. The libation that we customarily poured to the Old gods was not wasted.

3
The
Stang
as an
Altar

For some people, especially in Britain, witches and stangs are almost synonymous. Resembling a two-tined pitchfork, the stang displays the witch's fondness for items that are both useful in everyday life and symbolically meaningful. Representing the presence of the Horned God, it is usually a five or six-foot ash staff with a forked tine, but also serves as a handy 'thumb staff' when walking. Used by an individual witch or a working couple as an altar, the *'Stang'* becomes the symbol and Icon of the Horned God, as such it is treated with utmost respect. Naturally, individuals and Cuveens may vary somewhat in the meanings applied to the Stang within their tradition or method of working; and of course they will vary in how they 'dress' or garland it. In its pitchfork shape, the Stang typifies rural life. Anywhere livestock was kept would be found a fork for lifting and moving loose hay. No one would look twice at it, and only the initiate would recognize its additional meanings.

Even as the Christianity adopted the Bishop's Crosier from simple shepherd's crook, embellishing it with jewels and precious metals, so do witches often choose to embellish their personal staffs and the Cuveen Stang. One common addition is the totemic animal mask indicative of the Clan or 'gathering' that it is dedicated to. In the case of Cochrane's

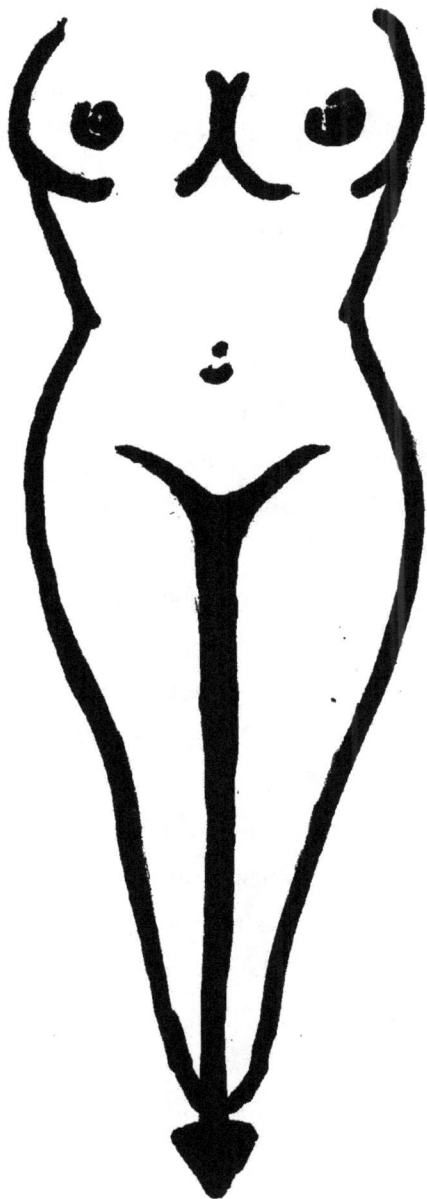

LADY STANG [AFTER JOHN]

old group, because we were the '*People of Goda of the Clan of Tubal Cain,*' we have our ram's head mask below the tines. Within the Clan of Tubal Cain, the Stang represents different aspects of the divine: of the Horned God, the Goddess, the sons and sacrificial twin year kings and of the woodland, the hunt and also of fertility.

The individual may therefore stand before their own Staff in effect, the priest-guardian of the sacred trees of Nemi to become a 'lineal descendent' of all those other priests and priestesses who once served the lonely shrines dedicated to the Old gods.[21] It is always in the care of the Maid, as it is she who is linked to it as the expression of the egregore or Clan soul. The Magister is linked to it at her behest. He holds it only if he is without a Maid, and should he die or be removed, then the Maid wields it until she has found another suitable Magister to gift it to.

When the entire Cuveen gathers before the Stang, both its potential and significance accelerate exponentially. It becomes a 'template' upon which we may write our ritual statement of intent. For example, placing a garland of grain stalks on the Stang, suggests thanksgiving to the Old Horn God and the Divine Creatrix[22] for the Harvest Home Gathering. If we were to weave yew twigs into this same garland, we would in effect, be mourning the harvest. Obviously, some small knowledge of symbolism is vital to ensure correct attributes are noted relevant to each rite. Outdoors the Stang may be driven into the ground;[23] but indoors, it may be sunk into a bucket of sand, with a small table or flat stone placed close to its base. A small bouquet of wild flowers or a solitary rose are placed upon the table together with a bottle of wine and a small chalice. Simplicity is the keynote.

The Stang's foot, traditionally shod with iron is a very old magical practice. Since the Stang is a consecrated magical tool, it stands to reason that its body will somehow retain some of the magical energy raised during its consecration. To the uninitiated eye, the magic of iron in particular, owes something to the 'secret' by which ancient ironworkers could convert what appeared to be mere stones into metal by treating them with fire. Another magical act would be perceived where the smith could take an iron bar and work it into a ploughshare, an axe, or sword; it is no wonder that the smith came to be regarded as a magician in his own right.[24]

That 'Magic counters Magic' is an ancient belief and from the evidence given during the 'Witch Trials,' there was a widespread belief that if someone was 'bewitched,' the way to break the spell was to draw blood from the person who had set the curse, using an iron knife, scissors, or nail. Thus the 'unnatural' magical iron would neutralize the natural magic of the spell. The presence of iron tools could supposedly (and literally) force shape-shifting witches back into human form and, when placed on the alleged witch's threshold, keep him or her from leaving the house in human or animal form. Even today, some Craft traditions forbid the presence of iron in the ritual circle. Obviously, having a smith-god as our tutelary deity, this does not apply to us.

When any Stang is consecrated, the magical power is drawn from the body of the 'Source' as She is better named. To prevent this power from draining back to Earth, the Stang's foot is shod with an iron ferrule, locking the energy into the shaft of the Stang. This can also be achieved by driving a nail partway into the foot of the Stang, then bending it over to form a bar. With iron at the top and bottom, we have changed an ordinary ash pole into a fully charged Stang, an effective altar, duly charged and consecrated.

Decorating the Stang:

Where the Stang is used in the sacred working area, on the periphery of the bounded circle, as opposed to its use as a walking stick or pitchfork, we decorate it in various symbolic ways, particularly at the common gatherings known by the following generic names: May's Eve, Lammastide/Harvest-Home, All Hallows' Eve and Candlemas. The garland will be different for each occasion, corresponding to that ritual's specific purpose and symbolism. Regardless of the season however, the Stang is always mounted with a pair of crossed arrows. The significance of these varies between traditions. Ours have intrinsic links to Neith and Astarte, both protective warrior goddesses.

The crossed arrows, like so much else in the Craft, combine practical function with symbolic meaning. Primarily, they provide support for the various garlands. They remind us that the Verdant Spirit of the forest is connected with the wild hunt and therefore death. In addition to this, they remind us of Herself in Dianic guise, - the Divine Huntress. Shot through by one of Her arrows, we are enamoured of Her forever. Filled with Her love, we cannot see a Full Moon without an overwhelming urge to be out in it in some quiet and lonely place. Without actually having to do or say anything, just stand there, allowing the moonlight and night breezes to work their magic, until all is in harmony and at one with the night and the hidden life around us. This is the essence of the Craft.

The arrows' colour also reveals much of relevance to us. In our tradition, the arrows may point up or down, dependent upon purpose. On the right as you face the Stang, this arrow is painted white, while the opposite arrow on the left, should be black. These colours refer to magical power and its usage. Simply put, the power raised from the shadow forces of the Old Ones during any rite is morally neutral; it is neither good nor bad. The worker of magics alone decides this; it is up to them to use or abuse it. There has always been a darker side to the Craft that may call upon the powers of chaos and disorder. Though these powers being rarely invoked remain latent, their place within the mysteries is assured.

So when two arrows are placed upon the Stang, we remember not just the Horn King, Himself a Devotee of Diana the Divine Huntress, but also that Source from where the compass draws its Virtue. In turn this reminds each of us of the responsibility that accompanies its generation and focus. Do we raise it in the name of spirituality, or just to raise Cain?

Although many traditions within the Craft divide their ritual year at May's Eve to All Hallow's Eve, still others place the death of the Old Year at All Hallow's and the beginning of the New at Candlemas, celebrated on or around February 2nd. The Clan, in accordance with medieval traditions, honour this descent into the Mound, but view the threshold, or turning tide as the peak, around Yule. The Old Fire is extinguished, prior to a new one being lit from its dying embers. The most appropriate garland for the Stang at this time would be yew twigs, which due to their extreme toxicity, should be handled with great care. In Britain, yews are common to churchyards. As a long-lived tree, they sometimes pre-date the graveyards they are rooted in. Additionally having further associations with weaponry (see note) the yew carries the symbolism of death and mourning. But conversely, the yew represents rebirth and reincarnation too, for its branches can grow downwards, take root, and eventually produce a new tree. So it then becomes our symbol of continuity of worship and spiritual development.

To reiterate then, for the May's Eve rite, the garland should ideally be composed of four primary woods; I would suggest: birch, hazel, thorn, and willow.[25] Birch often carries associations of youth and purification, generating good luck. Its presence emphasises the freshness and vibrancy of the reign of the Young Horn Child. Hazel has a long association with fire, fertility, divination, knowledge, and poetry. In the garland it reminds us that one of Her gifts is the 'Fire of Inspiration' that drives us to search for knowledge of the mysteries. Fertility can relate equally to both mind and body, suggesting the ability never to reject new ideas no matter where they come from and to take knowledge in the same open-minded way and to freely adapt it to our needs. The poetic and visionary arts as vehicles of inspiration need no elaboration for anyone familiar with mysticism.

Interestingly enough, English tradition says that hawthorn boughs 'protect against witchcraft' adding that they should never be taken indoors but instead fixed to door frames and lintels to induce good luck. Perhaps this notion of 'protection against witchcraft' concealed an earlier sacred meaning; at any rate, the Craft is replete with old country superstitions. In turn, we see the Thorn as the Old One's protection of the group against those who may wish its members harm. Willow has two traditional associations, with mourning and with water. Because willows grow best in moist places, they are considered sacred to the lunar aspect of Herself; the catkins also suggest the presence in the garland of mourning for the death of the Old Horn King.

May Eve is the most light-hearted festival, the time to 'sup the honey'd wine.' It derives its particular potency from the pheromonal activity of the woodlands, both in flora and fauna. The magically charged atmosphere is presided over by 'Robin' and 'Marian.'[26] Yet in the bowl afoot the hoof of the Stang, we place a mixture of milk, honey, and vinegar. The sweetness of the first two foods are countered by the bitterness of the third, demonstrating how life's joys are tempered by its sorrows and how a balance is always sought between them. This, we say, is what Fate had decreed for the year past, which we endured and celebrated with equal grace. At the close of the ritual, the Maid empties this bowl onto the ground, symbolically returning to the Source all the events, good and bad of the year past. At his peak now, the Young Horn King as verdant benefactor of abundance, triumphs over these previous adversities.

At Lammastide/Harvest-Home,[27] the obvious choice for garlanding the Stang would be the early harvest of first fruits and of various grains: wheat, rye, barley, oats and corn. Another choice could be a simple 'corn dolly,' a figure woven from the heads and stalks of ripe grain. Meadow flowers such as poppies would also be suitable. Traditionally, in the days of hand reaping by sickle or scythe, this 'dolly' was woven from the last sheaf of ripe grain cut by the reapers. Various customs existed for decorating and displaying the last sheaf, which had many nicknames.

According to folklore, as the grain was reaped, the 'spirit of the corn' kept moving ahead until 'She' was trapped in the last sheaf, which was then quickly bound to retain her spirit within. When the seeds were planted again in the spring sowing, the dolly and along with it the spirit of the Divine Creatrix was once again free to breathe life into the newly sown seed. As far as Robert Cochrane was concerned, what better place than the Stang upon which to hang a handful of quickly cut stalks, salvaged just before the blade reaps the final sheaf, that sanctuary wherein the spirit of the Goddess resides? Here the grain becomes a part of the altar to Her and to the Old Ones.

Some of us today plant grain in a pot at Candlemas and reap it at Lammas-tide for just this purpose. If everyone present then takes one of the seeds away with them for planting at home, when we have the Maid say:

"I am the plough to man's mind . . . I am the furrow wherein lies the seed,"

We recognize that our 'Faith' is inspired by the Divine Feminine and the seed we nourish and tend in the pot is no more than a symbol of our hoped-for spiritual growth in Her name. 'All Hallow's Eve' is when we remember our dead and light a candle to the memory of our ancestors. In this ritual we use two circles: one for the living and one for the dead.

Laid side by side, the circle for the dead touches the Northern point of the circle for the living. Beginning in the first circle the Rite then spirals into and back out of the second circle of the dead for the final part of the ceremony to take place. Given its significance, grain becomes appropriate for use upon the Hallows Stang if desired. After all, we do believe in rebirth for ourselves as well as for those who have 'crossed the river' ahead of us and does not yew symbolize this superbly?

Not all purpose in the Stang connects with seasonal rituals. When it is decorated with only the crossed arrows, without garland and with a sickle placed at its foot, the Stang represents yet another strand of the mythos of the Clan of Tubal Cain. It stands for the Dark King of the Underworld Mound, who, cloaked and hooded to hide his face and with broadsword in hand, stands ready to cut down his victims when the Fates have decreed that their souls are ready for harvesting. The sickle at the Stang's foot also reminds us that She now wears Her chillingly beautiful, yet fearsome Death Mask, and it is She who will, when the time is right:

"gather us up home again."

We say that in this configuration, the Stang becomes the Tau (T) and original Cross of sacrifice. Despite often conflicting research, it is now impossible to anchor the origins and practises of the 'sacrificial king' to any historical period; thus it remains a concept consigned to the realm of myth. Even so, it is an idea that has persisted for numerous centuries, and one that captivated the fertile imagination of Robert Cochrane who not only believed in it but lived it. He felt that should it 'necessary,' the High Priest, leader or Magister of the group should be willing to sacrifice himself to the Divine Feminine, the Source and Ultimate Creatrix in all Her forms and guises and to the Old gods for the good of the Clan.

Mythically speaking, we might think of a progression from the sacrificial Divine King concept whose manifest form morphed into that Virtue now embodied within the totemic 'animal.' Thus it becomes offered, that is 'given up' to each successive Clan leader to represent the once Incarnate God on Earth in their role of Magister.[28] In the ballad entitled the 'Witch Song' contained in one of Cochrane's letters to the late William Gray, an English ceremonial magician, we find these lines:

"There you and I, my love,
There you and I will lie
When the cross of resurrection is broken
And our time has come to die.
For no more is there weeping,
For no more is there death,
Only the golden sunset,
Only the golden rest."

Imagine a T-shaped cross hewn from the trunk of a living oak which has been left to rot in the place of sacrifice. No longer is it considered necessary that anyone or anything should give their life to mark the particular rite within our mythos that acknowledges the original 'sacrifice' of the gods that we might have life. Instead, a sickle is placed at the foot of the Clan Stang to invoke this archaic practice, symbolically recreating the mythos of the dying man/god on the Tau Cross. The Stang, when dressed with crossed arrows, knife and cup accompanies both skull and crossbones, and preferably absent of any garland, signifies this sacrificial death.[29] In death we must all face the Grim Reaper. Yet, for us we believe there is so much more to death than just dying.

Believing that our souls survive death and shift into rebirth many times, we mindfully work towards its release by cumulative gnosis at which point we attain spiritual unity with the Godhead. Here we see the Stang as an altar standing in the forecourt of an open tomb or burial mound.

To the left of the Stang resides the cup; the knife resides upon the right. Afore, the foot we place the skull and crossbones; and above these, the flame of spiritual inspiration burns brightly as earthly fire. Bearing individual significance, these objects change the overall meaning dependent upon the pattern they are presented in. The Cup or chalice as a sacred vessel has many esoteric connections with the Divine Feminine. Symbolising the Mother's Womb, it is the Cauldron of Inspiration, the magical vessel of several Northern European myths found within the Halls of the Castle of the Pale-Faced Goddess. Traditionally guarded by Nine Maidens (sometimes seven), it seethes with the wisdom of all ages. But to gain this knowledge, we must succumb to gestation trials within the shelter of the womb, followed by the birthing trauma both on physical and spiritual levels.

As the Cauldron of Life, the Chalice imparts the draft elixir, conferring the succour of rebirth or immortality upon the returning soul. Again, this idea has been recognized by many writers and students of occultism. In his book: *Rosicrucians: Their Rites and Mysteries,* first published in 1870, the writer Hargrave-Jennings states:

> "We claim the cauldron of the witches as in the original, the vase or urn of the fiery transmigration, in which all things of the world change."

In placing the cup to the left of the Stang as above, we observe yet another tradition. Since the knife embodies qualities relative to the masculine warrior whose right hand wields a sword, we instantly become aware of the shield held securely by his left hand. Another aspect of Herself alludes to that protective role which typifies a Mother for Her children: in this case – ourselves. An occult tradition asserts that the 'right-hand path' is the path of action, and the 'left-hand path' is of repose, which classically appeals to the mystical side of our natures. Thus when we describe Her 'mysteries' and ourselves as devotees in terms of the 'left-hand path,' we are boldly declaring our severance from orthodox convention and societal mores alien to Her liberating ideologies. We seek fulfilment beyond those restrictive parameters.

Finally, the Cup represents the old '*Sheela-na-Gig*' figures carved upon the lintels and doorways of some medieval churches. These depict the crude form of a naked squatting woman holding open her enlarged vulva. Within our mythos, we interpret this image as a beautiful woman whose nudity reveals a grinning skull where her vagina would be, conveying that through birth we are fated to die. Woman then, creates/generates life and also death.

At birth our individual life-spans are fixed: how we choose to apply ourselves between those two points is up to us. We may choose to waste the time given to us, in which case we will repeat a negative pattern into the next cycle; or we can follow the path of truth, where we may advance along the spiral path, gathering gnosis to carry forward into our next rebirth. If we choose to remain neutral and live a singular life with no thought of another one, then the soul remains fixed into that pattern unless something exceptional influences it. Where we learn nothing, we gain nothing, and so we are fated to remain on an endless round of existence. This again highlights Cochrane's premise that:

> "In fate and the overcoming of fate, lies the Grail. For from this inspiration comes and death is defeated. There is no fate so terrible that it cannot be overcome whether by the literal victory gained by action and in time, or the deeper victory of the spirit in the lonely battle of the self. Fate is the trial, the Castle Perilous in which we all meet to win or die. Therefore we are all concerned with fate, for humanity is greater than the gods, but not as great as the Goddess. When we triumph, fate stops and the gods are defeated, this is the

true meaning of magic. Both magic and religion are there to help us overcome Fate, and Fate is the hand that rocks the infant spirit." [30]

Returning to the Stang, to its right, the knife embodies all masculine virtue, both physical and mystical. Within our tradition it signifies the divine bridegroom in the sacred marriage counter-balancing the cup on the left, as bride. These two are symbols of the Maid and Magister used in the 'dedication' or '*Houzle*.'[31] Together they invoke the spirit of sacred union bound within their inherent sexuality, for when cup and knife are conjoined, they symbolise the coupling of the Maid and Magister acting as channels through which the primal energy of creation may flow.

On an individual level, the knife symbolizes personal will, by which impetus may attain access to increasing levels of spiritual advancement thereto experience alternate realities: the pleasures of a coven meeting, the trance-states of the shaman, including that of death as the soul reaches out and into the world beyond the River. The solitary witch reaches beyond the open tomb to find the secret of the '*Rose Beyond the Grave*,' to stand at the centre of the Castle in search of the Godhead. Three elements combine in Cup, Stang, and Knife to form our own triune Icon, expressing collectively the trinity of the Goddess, the Old Horned God, and the Young Horn King. As Cochrane used to say:

> "Feminine intuition coupled with masculine knowledge brings forth truth, which like the child, must be allowed to grow."

(It must be understood that these properties of intuition and knowledge are not restricted classifications of physicality but are elements of gender enjoyed by both sexes arbitrarily.)

Equally, it must be noted that the Stang itself becomes a symbol of this Sacred Trinity. After all, we are not devotees of a monolithic omnipotent Godhead; instead, we remind ourselves that the feminine aspects of divinity counterbalance those of the male and together they lead to the birth of Beauty - the Child of Wisdom. Returning again to the skull and crossbones, placed mindfully at the bottom of the Stang, we may also read a different narrative. For they additionally serve to describe a journey of the individual soul as it undergoes transformations within the *Faith*.

The first occurs when we either join a group or otherwise acknowledge the existence of the Goddess and the Old gods. Like the Holy Fool, we have stepped out upon that singular and straight path towards our salvation. Another transformation comes when we swear the Cuveen oath as a full member, becoming further masters of our own destinies. Within the Clan of Tubal Cain, the third and most important transformation occurs when we start to follow the path of the shaman-witch whose soul is trained in trance-working. Reaching out across the river and into the Otherworld, that soul defies the laws of the *'quick and the dead.'* It is precisely that same journey the soul must eventually take in death, the only difference being that each time the shaman-witch returns to this body and this world, his or her soul is the lighter for doing so.

Next we must consider the open tomb symbolizing the entrance to the Underworld used by the shaman while in trance. Reminiscent of a cave, we may liken it to the womb of the Great Mother, from whose body sprang the spirals of existence, and through which we may begin our spiritual argosies in earnest. By working the rite known as the 'Cave and Cauldron' we may garner some measure of our destinies. It was after all, in the darkness of caves that prehistoric people left evidence of their spiritual lives in the form of spectacular and evocative art, along with what appear to be shrines composed of skulls and bones.

While we can only guess as to their intentions, we may traverse the threads of our own mythical connections with the Old gods of Life along and through the winding maze of the Underworld, accessible via the symbols of cave, tomb, and womb. In summary, the Stang, whether actual or created as an image upon paper or cloth represents the total credo of birth, death, and rebirth central to our tradition. Any initiate seeing the Stang dressed with crossed arrows, cup and knife, or other tool for that matter, would know immediately what was meant, reading it as a living narrative even though this is more or less a shorthand version of a more elaborate original.

So when you look at a Witch's Stang, you in fact are viewing a theological statement in physical form. Robert Cochrane himself described the Stang thus in a letter to Bill Gray:

'Staff or Stang' - The Horse.

It is the supreme implement.

It represents the Middle Pillar of Yggdrasil.

The ash at one end, the rowan at the other.

Its roots are Malkuth or the Gateway, that is physical experience, and its top is the highest mystical experience.

It should be forked and bound at the base with iron.

The Gateway because it is phallic and represents Hermes the Guide and divides into the aspects as it rises.

The Moon, because it is the path to its mysteries - The foundation of Wisdom and spiritual experience.

It is Love because it represents the union of male and female, therefore attraction and counter-attraction, and it is Beauty, the Child of Wisdom (Horn Child).

It is Death, the final transformation.

The next attribute at the Horns is the Goddess or the primal movement.

In other words, it is a combination of masculine and feminine up to the position of death, then it becomes the single path of *Enlightenment.'*

4
Wyrd:
The
Pale-Faced
Goddess

One difference between the 'Clan of Tubal Cain' and many other forms of the Craft is that we take 'Fate' very seriously. But since the word 'Fate' has several meanings within common parlance, we refer to a distinct and particular use found in older Anglo-Saxon term: 'Wyrd.' Various Pagan cultures have perceived Wyrd or Fate as a single woman, sometimes as three women grouped to form a triplicity. Call Her the Spirit of Creation or the life force of the universe; to us She is the *Alpha-Omega of all Creation and Existence*. She is 'The Source' – its Wyrd in fact. Even the gods are considered subject to Her. Baldur, the beautiful and most beloved of the Norse gods was 'fated' to be killed by the one thing that had not taken the pledge to do him no harm, the mistletoe. Unlike most dying young gods of vegetation, fated to be born and killed over and over again, in the later Norse stories, Balder dies and is destroyed along with the heavens, the Earth, the gods, and mankind in the cataclysm the Norse called *Ragnarok*.

Many Pagan cultures throughout the archaic world similarly perceived 'Fate' as three sisters who spun, wove, then cut the thread of each person's life. To the Greeks, they were the 'Moirai,' named individually as *Clotho*,

Lachesis ('Getting by lot') and *Atropos* ('Irresistible'). Since a person's Fate was sometimes thought to be determined at birth, we hear an echo of this in the Roman names for these three sisters or *Parcae*: *Nona* ('nine-months birth'), *Decuma* ('ten-months birth') and *Morta* ('stillbirth').

To the Pagan Icelanders, the sisters were known as the '*Norns*,' named: *Urdr*, *Verdandi*, and *Skuld*. In the Anglo-Saxon stories, however, the names of two sisters are lost, leaving only 'Wyrd,' the name by which their fateful trio is commonly known. In one story, they live in a cavern by a white well and are presented as daughters of the Goddess Night. This concept has, for many, led to their comparison with the three main visible phases of the Moon.

At the New Moon they weave a new individual Fate; the Full Moon represents this moment in the 'now' where the sisters temporarily anchor. At the Waning Moon, they weave the individual's final doom. It is common for those of us in the Craft to say we are drawn to it instinctively: our destiny realises that the presentation of 'choice' in swearing to follow the way of the Old Horned God and the Goddess must always be a matter of '**Faith**'. Therefore, if we dedicate ourselves to the Old Ones, we become fated to doom ourselves in seeking the elusive Moon Queen and her Horned Consort in the hidden places concealed under the cloak of the Goddess Night.

We meet the three sisters again in Shakespeare's infamous Scottish play, the much lauded Macbeth. In the first act, when Macbeth is still King Duncan's victorious war leader, he meets the three witches on the heath and they great him:

First witch: *"All hail, Macbeth! hail to thee, thane of Glamis!"*
Second witch: *"All hail, Macbeth! hail to thee, thane of Cawdor!"*
Third witch: *"All hail, Macbeth that shalt be king hereafter!"*

They have named his previous noble title, his new title, the Thane of Cawdor, gained when its rebellious former holder was executed; and the title that he does not yet have. If we understand these three hags as the 'Wyrd,' then they have just revealed Macbeth's past, present, and future in chronological order. Perhaps when Shakespeare was writing this, a common oral tradition still existed for him to draw upon, even though by the sixteenth century the three sisters of the Wyrd became caricatured as 'witches.' Despite this, their prophetic roles remained: they could forecast past, present, and future. Robert Cochrane was convinced that Shakespeare *"knew something."* In a letter to William Gray he wrote:

> "Shakespeare really knew his witchcraft. I have a wild theory that he spent some time in one of the more advanced clans; and that it was during his service that he first gave birth to the silver tongue."

In the Clan, the 'Wyrd' as a lone sister carries many of the attributes of the Pale-Faced Goddess. She seems as old as time itself, and Her face is visualized as white and cold as newly fallen snow. No furrow marks Her brow; no blemish mars her flawless, inestimable beauty. Her glossy hair, of ebon' night hangs long, framing her perfectly oval face. Hypnotic blue eyes, cold as ice, stare ambivalently out from beneath fine black curving eyebrows. Her nose is slightly hooked, almost beak-like above full, sensuous blood red lips. Her half-smile reminds us that She is the one who lines Her nest with the bones of poets and others who have fallen under the love spell of Her lunar magic.[32]

In this guise, She keeps the Cauldron into which is invested all the attributes of Wyrd. Central symbol of numerous Craft traditions, the Cauldron is the vessel of wisdom and inspiration containing past, present, and future knowledge. When we drink from the Cauldron, we hope, like Gwion Bach to gain some measure of knowledge. The Cauldron symbolically contains the medium of generation in the form of new ideas. Though formless and unexpressed, they remain potent with the promise of knowledge to be gained by those souls thirsty enough to drink from Her Cauldron. We therefore look upon it as the mystical pool of existence. It holds in suspension life past and life yet to come; we return to it in death to await our eventual rebirth from this pool, whence we face life anew with all its triumphs and tribulations.

We portray the Goddess (Gaude/Guiden) seated on a throne with two of Her sacred geese, one at either side, looking up at Her, as do we, with adoring eyes. She sits calmly, dispassionate and infinitely remote, with an air of detached sadness tinged with compassion. For She is the one who knows the ultimate Fate of our world because She is the one who ordained its weaving into the very fabric of creation. Even when that Fate finally has been played out, She will still be there, the Alpha/Omega of *all* Creation.

5
The
Spirals
o f
Existence

O f all witchcraft symbols, the 'Spiral Dance' or 'Spiral Path' is perhaps the most enigmatic. During the sixth decade of the 20th century, when the modern Craft's growth spurt began, all that many of us really knew about this phenomenon, was that the old-time witches used spiral dances as part of their rites for trance inducement. These were possibly a variation or form of the many circle dances preserved within the greater body of 'folk' tradition. Over time, many theories have been advanced that attempt to explain their enigmatic purpose. Based upon some of these ideas, Robert Cochrane instigated the possibility of a spiral dance or path to be performed in such a way that it would fit sympathetically into the Clan's mythos. Unfortunately, he did not complete this before his death, and so this task weighed upon the shoulders of those he left behind; finally, it has achieved considerable success.

Within the Clan of Tubal Cain, the spiral motif has been developed into what we call 'The Spirals of Existence.' We see the spiralling path as illustrative of the enduring soul's journey of death and re-incarnation, until we break free of its repetitive cycle. This spiral path of wisdom explains only part of an ancient human belief in the interplay between natural and supernatural events that has long shaped and controlled humankind's life upon this rich Earth. It is a belief older than memory and one the Craft has re-envisioned.

But in reviving it, did we fully understand what we had taken on board? The world of our ancestors was a different, far less secure world than our own. Whereas ours is heavily populated; theirs, by contrast, was sparsely so. No technology or infra-structure to detract the mind from its musings and contemplations; yet instead, a world soothed only by the warmth of the daytime Sun existed that often seemed hostile and inimical even to life itself. At night, faced with darkness that in our light saturation we may never comprehend, they were able to see the heavens illuminated by billions of stars, shining brilliantly against the pitch-black vaulted arc of the skies until the rising of the Moon cast a cold, harsh, twilight over the land. Little wonder that this celestial mirror came to symbolize the Old White Goddess Herself.

Faced night after night with this phenomenon of a brilliance and intensity such as we rarely experience, it is no surprise that they sought more than mere bodily existence, and a reason for our existence. Today, no matter how slight or vague our beliefs, we are all familiar with the concept of the immortal soul as a separate entity from the mortal body. Most religions teach this to their followers from an early age. After all, how many of us would really choose to accept that there is absolutely nothing beyond the end of this life?

The circle and its geometric relative the spiral are among the oldest of all religious symbols. Psychologists see the circle as symbolizing the total Self, not just 'I,' but all the usually hidden parts of ourselves as well. At its most basic level, the ritual area, typically worked within the Craft, is that which follows an archaic paten – the circle. Marked for the cardinal points, now commonly associated with the four elements of fire, earth, air, and water, we become suspended in liminal time. In addition, the circle marks delineates the ritual area from that of the mundane, giving us liminal space. Its shape suggests two patterns of movement: deosil (clockwise/sunwise) and widdershins (anti-clockwise). Southern Hemisphere practitioners often reverse these because for them the Sun's apparent path through the sky, which gives us the word 'deosil' (sunwise), is obviously anti-clockwise.

Within the tradition of the Clan of Tubal Cain, we consider deosil movement to be celebratory. It moves with the dance of life, following the *apparent* motion of the Sun. Thus we associate it with living and enjoyment. On the other hand, when we 'pace the Mill' in a widdershins direction, we are actively working to magical ends and invoking supernatural powers.

Another intriguing speculation connected with the geometry of the circle involves a possibly natural phenomenon, that of 'corn circles.' Mysterious circular patterns found mainly in fields of grain in Britain and elsewhere, range from simple designs to exquisitely complex fractals. While many of the more elaborate patterns publicized in recent years were apparently made by people, some simpler corn circles do seem to be caused by whirling columns of air. We know that circa 2,500BCE, burial customs changed in Britain. Instead of mounding earth over long barrows, a shift occurred for a short time towards the formation of round or oval mounds over shallow graves. Excavations have revealed that many of these barrows were built over mature areas of grass and even over cultivated fields. Perhaps something significant occurred at some point that marked these particular locations as special?

But if some visible, impressive phenomenon had occurred, how would this have been perceived by Bronze Age peoples? Would they think that the gods had 'breathed' on that very spot - creating a whirlwind that left behind a visible sacred mark? This is quite possible, though we have no way of knowing. So, without endorsing some of the wilder theories concerning 'crop circles' today, we may speculate that it could simply have been a naturally formed crop circle that influenced those peoples, finding some particular significance therein that caused them to dedicate the eternal resting places of their dead in like fashion. As if to endorse the importance of the circle, many great stones bear the spiral motif carved upon them, along with those aptly named – 'cup and ring.'

Such potent imagery marks the subconscious indelibly, influencing revived and modern practises. For our 'All Hallow's' ritual, two circles lay side by side representing the living and the dead. We begin moving deosil out of one circle, moving widdershins into that consigned to the dead, before finally returning deosil into the circle of life. Since 'All Hallow's Eve' or Samhain is our time for honouring and remembering the dead, the transition from one circle to the other draws on the afore-mentioned principles. We illustrate this concept graphically with an outwardly spiralling circle that eventually turns in on itself, leading to death, where it becomes the *Rose Beyond the Grave'* and the spiral path of the re-incarnating soul.

Within the Clan of Tubal Cain, we uphold the concept of the returning soul, itself a fragmented seed, a spark of primal divinity progressing slowly along an inwardly spirally path until it reaches the point of no return. Here it unites with the Source to illustrate how we begin that journey anew from the edge, the periphery and farthest from the point, the qutub centre and core of existence. Here the World Soul draws us towards itself, guiding all those willing to make that first tentative step. Before this, our souls progress unknowingly along the path to the point where we start to recall past lives. From then on, our spiritual destinies lie within our own hands.[33] Our Craft tradition teaches that the further we go along this path, the more we gain in spiritual knowledge, but this in itself is not enough. We must learn to balance knowledge with wisdom, because the further along the path we are, the greater the potential for abuse exists. Here I do not mean 'accidental' abuse that may occur through lack of understanding, but the deliberate intention to garner a sheer naked lust for power.[34]

As a concept, the spiral-path concept is not solely aligned to Craft teaching. Its Virtue reaches beyond the boundaries of the *'Faith,'* to almost universal application. Especially within other occult traditions. In the work of Valentinus, a second century Gnostic Christian teacher, we find the same concept expressed through the metaphor of a hill with an upward winding road going around and around it leading to its summit. Along the road the traveller discovers certain symbols, each representing a task or obstacle the initiate must overcome before he or she reaches the apex. The prize for reaching the apex is that which replaces *'Faith'* with the gnosis of certainty concerning the existence of the Godhead and the true relationship between it and Humanity.

Even though the symbols are often different between traditions, the same basic idea of progression along a spiral path until we come face to face with that Godhead remains. The double-ended spiral may be perceived as also being emblematic of re-incarnation, the opening spiral of life adjoined to the closing spiral of death. Despite such a lengthy discussion on the concepts of death, it would be incorrect to assume an obsession with it. On the contrary, within the Craft, we honour and celebrate the glorious gift of life. But we must not allow that to distract us from the greater goal. Convinced that behind life there is something other than mere bodily death, we also acknowledge that life is not always sweet and we must live out each life as it is given to the best of our capabilities, accepting what it has to offer while at the same time embracing its spiritual dimension. The Pagan emperor Marcus Aurelius was both wise and blessed when he prayed thusly:

"All is in harmony with me that is in harmony with you, O Universe."

This spiritual element demands far more commitment from us than an occasional acknowledgement. It demands the belief that our rebirth and future lives are governed by what we do in this life. Looking at the world today, being reborn into it can give a whole new meaning to the word 'Hell.' Many people sadly believe themselves to be in hell on Earth now, with little hope of changing it. Nor do we support the idea of a reward in Paradise or Heaven, as some religions teach. Instead, we believe our spiritual salvation is in our own hands to the extent that what we do in this life determines the Fate of the next. Because we are by default that which we think ourselves to be, unless we use our knowledge wisely, we fail to shift forwards on the spiral, returning, to begin again from that same point. Hence one of the basic teachings of the Craft is sometimes summarized as 'The Law of Threefold Return' which has no connection to the Wiccan tenet of the same title.[35]

More than 1,300 years ago, the Anglo-Saxon monks of Lindisfarne created a book now recognized as one of the greatest treasures of the British Library, named appropriately, the Lindisfarne Gospels. The title page of each gospel is beautifully illuminated, decorated with complex designs entwined around with the exquisitely handwritten letters. True to the old tradition that only God was permitted perfection in creation, each of these illustrated title pages has somewhere in its intricate patterns a little piece of unfinished work. Usually something minor, such as a feather upon a bird's wing, each scribe would wisely withhold.

But there is one exception; in the lower right-hand corner of the title page to Gospel of St. Matthew, the design has been deliberately 'spoiled' by the inclusion of a small spiral at the end of one of the arms of interlaced designs. No one knows why this spiral was introduced, as it would have been just as easy to leave something unfinished as with the other three gospels. We know that a monk named Eadfrith was the artist and writer, but we should also realize that he was no more than four or five generations away from his decidedly Pagan ancestors. We must wonder whether he included the spiral to satisfy artistic gratification, or was he recording something of deep rooted significance, something that did not conflict with his fledgling Faith?

6

Elementals, Watchers, and the Shadow Company

As a matter of historical interest, some English ceremonial magicians made a serious attempt to raise an elemental spirit in 1857CE on a rooftop in London's Oxford Street. They were members of an occult club founded by Edward George Bulwer-Lytton, a Victorian novelist famous for *'Zanoni'* and *'The Last Days of Pompeii.'* Bulwer-Lytton was no mere dabbler in the occult arts. His letters show that he was a Rosicrucian, and if Helena Blavatsky, the founder of Theosophy is to be believed, he truly belonged to the Brotherhood of Adepts. Aside from notorious incidents like this, an encounter with an elemental is generally more subtle. In another of his letters to the late William G. Gray, written in the mid-1960s, Robert Cochrane half-jokingly mentioned what he called 'nature spooks,' going on to remark:

> "Once you have achieved your (ritual working) purpose, leave everything as you found it, or else you will spend some uncomfortable nights with nature spooks clumping round your room taking it out on you for disturbing them. They are elementals and know not

conscience as we know it. However, they can be tamed and kept by you as a friend. My family has had one for years and he delights in practical jokes. According to how he has been used, so he has become, and I think Tomkins was used unnecessarily for tangle-foot work."

The remainder of the letter continues, much in the same vein. People hearing this for the first time must think as we did, somewhat sceptically! Those of us who visited Cochrane's house remember an ornamental brass plate hung on the wall. On many occasions, while we sat and talked, four distinct and clear pings would sound on this plate. He would look up, smile, and say:

"Tomkins is around again."

Now this plain and unremarkable wall stretched from the back to the front of the house, whose vast expanse was broken only by the plate hung approximately near its middle; there was absolutely no obvious way the plate could be made to ping. So the only logical conclusion one could draw was that it was either 'Tomkins' at work, or something else was making the noise, and one that none of us could determine or explain how it could be achieved. And believe me, we tried.

Cochrane maintained, and I have no cause to contradict him, that indoor meetings differ qualitatively from outdoor meetings. Rituals performed outdoors not only immerse you within the presence of nature elementals, but may occasionally manifest before you as small flashes of blue-green lights around the working site: a sure sign of elemental presence. No one can say authoritatively just what elementals are, but we do not believe those who explain these as 'fireflies' or 'static electricity.' Experienced workers will see these flashes in weather too cold for any insect activity. As for the 'static electricity' explanation, why then are the flashes more common outdoors, rather than indoors, as would be expected? Furthermore, static electricity does not have the habit of flitting from bush to bush for a good four or five minutes at a time.

The simplest explanation might be to say that elementals are the lowest form of spirit energy generated by every living thing. If a tree, bush, or plant is living, growing, and seeding itself, then within it must be some of the same life force that is within us. Just as we emanate an auric field, so do they, perceived most frequently as intermittent flashes of light at play in the woods at night as a physical manifestation of their presence.

Except for the odd cases in which an elemental has attached itself to a family, you almost never get elemental activity indoors, nor even the atmosphere associated with elemental activity. Certainly some buildings can give out psychic impressions and have a psychic atmosphere of their own, but that is not the same thing. The uses to which the building has been exposed and the emotive responses of the people living or working within them create those impressions and may be easily picked up by sensitive persons or empaths.

Another point worth noting is that certain places can be psychically dead. Any rite worked there will simply fall flat, void of any elemental activity. But most of us accustomed to outdoor ritual work are more than familiar with elemental activity. As our hackles rise, we recognize the feeling of being constantly watched while ever we remain on the ritual site. We become prepared for the constant tripping over something that is not there, the things that end up in different places from where they were put. In short, all the small but annoying things that appear to go wrong at certain gatherings. Some of these can of course be explained as carelessness, but there are others that can only be blamed upon elemental activity, or as they once were known, the mischievous woodland sprites.

You may naturally be wondering why these 'sprites' would bother anyone in attendance to the Divine Creatrix? Why not pester people whose motives are less reverent? (How do you know that they don't?) Quite simply, as elementals are among the most basic spirit-energy forms, they belong more properly to the forces of chaos than those of order. Being what they are, they actually can resent our presence in what is essentially their world. Lacking the faculty of logic, they cannot act but only react against what they instinctively feel is an intrusive presence. This manifests as disruption. Elementals though amoral, are not dangerous, merely annoying. Ignoring them and using the same site repeatedly will gradually lessen their responses, as they slowly come to accept your presence among them. On the positive side, the presence of elementals confirms the site as a geomantic hot-spot. The wilder and more magically potent the site, the more likely you are to find them. Conversely, the nearer you are to civilization, the weaker their influence.

When we try to control nature and shape it to our needs, we also reshape our landscape, and in doing so, we force these nature elementals deeper and deeper into the wilds, beyond normal bounds. Our activities end up pushing the very spirit of nature further from mundane life. One way that we may entice the wild back from these remote areas, is to plant a truly wild garden, planted up with indigenous species, and left for nature to re-claim. And so when you pour a libation for the Old Ones, why not spare a few drops for the elemental woodland sprites that haunt the place where you are working, out of respect for them and to acknowledge their presence as one not only invited, but desired.

A belief in 'the watchers' is another facet of the Craft. Any serious student of witchcraft will know that the one place where witches of old were accused of gathering, was within a churchyard. And most certainly in the fourteenth, fifteenth, or even sixteenth centuries, no person other than a witch would wish to linger in a graveyard at night. During the hours of darkness, the bone-yards were reputedly the haunt of the Devil, and his horde of assorted demons, ghosts, spooks, and all things that shriek and go bump in the night. But to the earlier Northern European pagan mind, the graveyard was not thus considered to be a nocturnal place of fear and dread, but simply one that concedes its supernatural inhabitants. Included among these are the shades of both ancestors and its guardians, as in the afore mentioned 'watchers.'

These spectral sentinels are obliged to this role as the last person buried there; they are bound in duty to do what they can to guard the graves against desecration, not in a physical sense such as knocking someone down, but supernaturally, generating runs of 'bad luck,' bad health, unsettled dreams, and all the things that bring unease to the soul. In fact, medieval occultists looked upon burial grounds as the sacred earthly dwelling place wherein ancestral spirits could be consulted about family concerns within the Clanship and about what the future may hold for them. Taking too much on 'Faith' runs contra to the general ethos of the Craft; after all, the last thing we need is to become hidebound and trapped in dogma.

So it is up to each individual to decide whether or not to accept the existence of the 'watchers.' But do first spend the witching hours in a graveyard with a friend; then decide if the 'watchers' exist or not. The 'Shadow Company' or the 'Hooded Ones' [*Cuccilatii*] are contemporary terms for an old phenomenon, the ancestral guardian spirits of both Cuveen and Clan. Some believe the 'Shadow Company' is the departed souls of past witches attracted back to this world by the workings of others. Some will say they are souls who have progressed through many incarnations and may no longer return to this Earth in carnate form. They dwell instead upon the plane of 'Gwynvyd'. Within the Clan of Tubal Cain we are more inclined to the first definition. Whichever definition you adopt, you may be sure that they exist.

Christianity however, inherited much of the lore and tradition of Classical Roman paganism, which looked upon death as unclean and taboo. To the pagan Romans, death was a pollutant - an attitude much of Western culture has inherited. Even medieval Christianity with its reliquary cult of 'saintly' bones of martyrs as objects of veneration has not eradicated this distaste for the graveyard after dark. Our Anglo-Saxon pagan relatives did not fear the dead but viewed them rather as honoured ancestors, consulting them often, particularly in times of need.

Sharing similar beliefs to these and other people around the world, ancestral souls were deemed to retain an active interest in the wellbeing of their Clan or family group despite having passed over into the Otherworld. Without one's family, who would make offerings to feed their souls in the Otherworld? We can easily understand that where certain rites were worked among the corpse mounds and churchyard, it is highly unlikely that summoning the Devil or legions of imps and evil spirits just to plague their neighbours would have been a consideration; nor indeed is it likely they would have entertained any notion of desecration of family cemeteries. Their purpose lay in contacting not demons, but ancestral shades (a practise strictly forbidden by the Church) in the hope that their miserable lot could be marginally improved upon. If this meant putting curses and other magical spells on their oppressors, then so be it.

In the New World, because Christianity arrived much later than in Europe, we can demonstrate another parallel in the 'Mexican Day of the Dead,' a festival held on November 2nd featuring candy-sugar skulls, 'pan des muertos' (bread of the dead), and toy skeletons of clay and wood.

Traditionally, the family will gather around a table constructed as a crude shrine to the ancestors lit by candles and heaving with offerings of food, flowers, candles, alcohol and thick, rich, sticky hot chocolate beloved of the old Aztec upper classes. On the evening of the next day, all family members then gather around family graves decorated with lit candles and flowers, so that everyone could feast, eating and drinking while listening to uplifting and riotous brass band music. In England this would naturally be considered an act of sacrilege and desecration.

A European way of 'feeding' ancestral shades that survived Christianity was in the Italian custom of preparing the *'fave dei morti'* or 'beans of the dead'[36] as a special treat to be eaten on All Souls Day. Today a small piece of sweet pastry replaces the bean, but the custom concerning the humble bean is still held there. According to Classical myth, the Goddess Demeter was the Goddess of all vegetation except the bean. Because it was not under her influence, the bean gradually became looked upon as a suitable funerary offering and with time came to be considered as holding the souls of the dead within it. This may be one reason why the Greek philosopher Pythagoras enigmatically forbade his disciples to eat beans. Anyone wishing to do something special for the feast after the 'All Hallow's Eve' ritual could easily prepare for their gathering these 'beans' of the dead.

In a letter written to the occultist William Gray, Robert Cochrane refers to his firm belief that the soul of a witch returns from across the 'river' to reclaim the 'quick,' moving on to other lives. The nearest thing that we have to a common experience of death is literally, the Near-Death Experience (NDE), which has been extensively studied by many researchers. Some of these researchers claim to see a common pattern in the NDE. Often the person concerned becomes detached from his or her suffering and seems to have the ability to watch over whatever trauma has induced that state. Next, the sensation of falling or being sucked through a long dark tunnel towards a grid of light is noted. In many cases, after this, the experience involves being met by someone known to that person who leads them towards a blinding light.

Finally and perhaps unwillingly, the person may then find themselves forced back through the tunnel, into their bodies because it is not yet their allotted time to die. Important common elements linking NDEs include the experience of a conscious existence beyond the point of death plus the absence of an abrupt severance between the body and its soul. Clearly, many old Pagans accepted these as facts, hence the many elaborate funerary rites designed to separate the soul from its body, sending it securely on its way into the Otherworld. So if we do accept the existence of a sentient 'soul' after death, we must logically accept that a soul should then be capable of returning to this world. And with the concept of reincarnation comes the soul's journey along the spiral path. The further along the path it is, the more spiritually advanced it will be. Hence Cochrane's [original] comment that:

"Now around the Castle winds the River or Time. It is this that distinguishes us from the quick (living) and the dead . . . It is also the beginning of power and distinguishing mark between a witch and a pagan, since the witch crosses the River [while] a pagan remains with the quick."[37]

But why should the soul of a witch be different from any other soul? In a sense, of course it is not, but a key work within the Craft is that which 'trains' the soul to knowingly enter its reincarnation rather than an unknown rebirth. This unknown state is likened to death, or sleep. So we have to ask: does Valhalla, Paradise or Heaven exist as the eternal resting places for millions of souls? And is there yet another resting place along the spiral path from whence the unknowing soul is reborn time and time again until it becomes spiritually aware of the spiral path to the Godhead for all such seeking souls to find? This is the mystery Robert Cochrane expressed through the lines where:

"that desire to survive created the pathway into the Otherworld."

From this, the souls of witches are able to find their way 'home' again, responding:

"like to like and blood to blood."

7
Child's
Play?

One of the more famous and enigmatic of his riddles expresses perfectly the working ethos of the Clan and the procedure for ritual.

"This is the taper that lights the way,

This is the cloak that covers the stone,

That sharpens the knife.

That cuts the cord,

That binds the Staff,

That's owned by the Maid,

Who tends the fire,

That boils the pot,

That scalds the sword,

That fashions the bridge,

That crosses the ditch,

That compasses the hand,

That knocks the door,

That fetches the watch,

That releases the man,

That turns the Mill,

That grinds the corn,

That makes the cake,

That feeds the hound,

That guards the gate

That hides the maze

That's worth a light

And into the castle that Jack built."

We do not entirely know where this rhyme came from. Some say Robert Cochrane wrote it himself modelling it on the well-known nursery rhyme: 'This is the house that Jack built.' Others believe that it was handed down through his family. Though he never actually claimed to have written it himself, more than once he said to people that:

"nothing concerning the Craft should ever be stated definitively"

He then went on to bring in what he called areas of 'grey magic.' One goal of grey magic was simply to deliberately cloud these issues of age or authenticity, sending people away not knowing precisely what he did or did not believe in, or what he had actually said in the first place. You could say that he loved mystery for its own sake, which is not quite the same thing as saying that male bovine excrement baffles brain - despite what some people thought of his approach!

Whatever its source, this particular rhyme is a major example of an old witch tradition, fully endorsed by Cochrane, of wrapping teachings and beliefs up in such a way that only someone *already* aware could understand what was actually being said. At first you might think you were reading or hearing something that belonged on the school playground, not to a witch tradition, and thus the **'Faith'** is easily concealed from outsiders, yet easily revealed to initiates, with the skills and keys to understand the real meaning. Such has the approach to the mysteries ever been guarded the world over.[38]

True, this 'cloaking of teaching' can lead to exploitation by fraudulent teachers but it nevertheless retains its value as 'connected' methodology of inspiration and intuition. Sadly, many people remain unable to fully digest the essence of the mysteries until they are 'made ready.'[39] Much of Cochrane's 'system' certainly seems to have been devoted to testing that state of readiness. Such seemingly simple rhymes could also be tests of knowledge, questions along the lines of the old riddle:

"How many beans make five?"

Put the question to the person and they must answer within the context of the rhyme or riddle on the relevant point of faith. So let us now turn to this particular 'childish rhyme.'

The *"taper that lights the way"* could be seen as the light that shows the path on the way to and from the ritual working site. In fact, it refers specifically to the *"soul candle,"* lit when forging their oaths during admittance into the Clan. The candle symbolizes the soul and the inner light of inspiration that leads a person first to recognize and to then seek knowledge within the Circle of mysteries. When that oath is taken, the aspirant steps out upon the path that ultimately leads to the Spinning Castle of the Old Goddess. The light that guides them through the darkness of all doubt and uncertainty is truth and the search for that truth.

With the line *"This is the cloak that covers the stone,"* Cochrane referred poetically to the Goddess Night under whose darkness our workings are hidden. Night similarly covers the whetstone, another symbol used by the Magister alongside a steel-bladed knife to strike a few token sparks over the main fire before it is lit. Whetstones were associated by the Norse and Anglo-Saxons with Thunor/Thor, the God with power of lightning and fire. The most famous whetstone of all was found among the grave-goods of a seventh century East Anglian king at the famous 'Sutton Hoo' longboat burial site. This long, slim stone, surmounted by the figure of a stag had never been used to sharpen sword or axe but served instead as an emblem of royal power. It probably rested on the king's knee during certain ceremonies, in like manner of the sceptre.

After this, the next set of lines, *"That sharpens the knife/That cuts the cord/That binds the Staff/That's owned by the Maid,"* refer specifically to the Goddess or Divine Creatrix in the aspect of the Mother giving birth to the Young Horn Child. When the umbilical cord is cut, the Young Horn King becomes independent and able to follow his own fate. The Old Winter King is now dead, and the Young Summer King rules in his stead. The mystery is expressed through the 'Mother' appearing now as the eager 'Maid' awaiting Her new lover.[40] Maid and Young King join and in doing so, turn the age-old cycle of life with its promise of birth and rebirth.

"That binds the Staff"

This describes how we equate the Cuveen Stang with the Young King (proving that this development of a concept is more recent than some people were led to believe). Traditionally, the Magister is looked upon as the manifest representative of the Old Horned God via the gift of Virtue with the Cuveen Stang regarded as indicative of this office. Of necessity he became looked upon as the priest/leader of the group, transforming the Stang into an Icon of the Old Horn/ed God and the Young Horn (Twin Year) Kings. So the 'bound' Staff represents the *unborn child*, and by cutting the cord that binds it, the spirit of the Young King is released from the womb of the Mother.

The next five linked lines refer to what we call the '*Old Covenant*.' The Maid is she who by this singular and sacred Rite becomes in our eyes the Bride of the Old Horned God through his representative on Earth - the Master/Magister or Devil. Divine in her own right, she is no less than a 'living representative of the Goddess' to whom all offer homage and care of their soul. You will recall, it is she that *"tends the fire,"* placing her in the category of *"keeper of the hearth fire,"* the one who serves the congregation from the cauldron after pouring the libation. She therefore grants permission for 'Her' cauldron and hearth fire to be used for the rite. But, were she so inclined, she could bring the whole ritual to an abrupt end by overturning the pot and putting out the fire. No one would doubt or question her reasons for doing so. The poem continues:

"That boils the pot/
That scalds the sword/
That fashions the bridge/
That crosses the moat..."

When four men come into the circle to 'hallow the quarters,' they plunge a sword into the cauldron - hence the expression: *"scalding the sword."* Afterwards, it is handed to the Summoner, who then takes it to the edge of the circle at the North point to form the X-bridge on the edge of the circle with the besom or as it is sometimes called, the 'ditch' or 'moat.'

Next is the enigmatic line, *"That compasses the hand,"* which in this case is the 'hand of power.' Shown with a pointing forefinger, it is commonly fashioned onto the hilt of numerous coven swords for particular ritual use where the focus of power was directed towards a certain location; here the sword acts as a wand/staff. This 'power' must of course derive somewhere, and in our tradition, it is sourced from the Pale-Faced Goddess who presides over the Castle and the Cauldron. This mythos places the Castle in a nebulous Otherworld, of lands to the far North of eternal ice and snow, and from whence chilling winds bring Death, the final transformation. When magnetic compasses first began usage in the European Middle Ages, it must have seemed magical that a lodestone always points North. No one knew quite how or why magnetism worked, but its mystery resides in the sky above, confirmed by the still point or axis of the Nowl/North Star.

The ritual outline continues with the lines:
"That knocks the door/
That fetches the watch/
That releases the man."

Even as the doorkeeper once tapped out a rhythm on the floor with his staff (of office) to announce the presence of a visitor to the Lord's Hall, so too does the Magister in like fashion within the working area or circle. Facing North, he must tap the foot of the Stang on the ground three times knocking symbolically on the door that separates this world from the Otherworld. After this, all participants should become aware of the presence of the Shadow Company, which is felt more than 'seen.' Gathering at the boundaries of working areas to form the *"watch"* they signify a continuity of the once prevalent nocturnal community guard. This 'personage' whom they release is none other than the Old Horned God himself, through his own symbol - the Totemic ram upon the Cuveen Stang. In other words, his spirit is awakened so that he may dutifully take his position behind the Stang; there, all worship offered recognizes the potent force behind that symbol.

Following that are the lines:

"That turns the Mill/That grinds the corn/That makes the cake."

These describe the widdershins pacing of the witches during each magical working. The *"corn"* represents the individual cuveeners and their collective aims and ritual intent. As grains are ground into flour, so the individual persons become subsumed within the whole as the Mill is paced, grinding together their common purpose. The *"cake"* symbolizes that ritual purpose, be it a healing, a cursing, or whatever. It then becomes an act of worship offered in exchange for supernatural aid from the ancestral shades, known as the 'Old Ones,' leading to the next couplet:

"That feeds the hound/That guards the gate."

Every gate has its guardian, or at least every gate that guards anything worth having does. As the instrument of Her will, the hound, in effect judges the sincerity of the worship embodied within the rite. And where we might suggest that the 'hound turned up his nose at the cake,' we are actually saying that the Old gods refused to grant what was asked of them in ritual. The 'gate' guarded by the hound stands in front of the *"Hidden Maze,"* and here again we meet one of the most basic concepts of this mystery tradition within the Craft. It concerns the creation of a home within the Otherworld. This *"Maze"* is a hidden path through the Otherworld leading symbolically to a river complete with a ferry to cross it. On the other side the path continues to a rocky mount where we find:

"the Castle that spins without motion between two worlds."

Thinking of that Castle, the line:

"And into the house that Jack built."

94

THE STAR CROSSED SERPENT

We can begin to merge these principles into some measure of clarity, for '*Jack-in-the-bush*' is a popular folkloric version of the sacrificed king, the dying spirit of the Old God/King reborn within and through the Young Horn King. The blood of countless willing 'sacrifices' binds the Castle's walls, and its foundations stand on the once living bones of poets, bards, and prophets. Hence: "*the house that Jack built*" means the home of the Pale-Faced Goddess of both life and death, and for us, the place of refuge and rebirth.[41] By taking our place in the circle and working the rites of the Old gods, we hope to gain access to this Sanctuary. The Castle is built from all acts of worship and all rites performed over centuries in their honour. In conclusion, the final and most important line of all describes no less than an oath:

"That's worth a light."

When a person takes an oath during full admission into the Clan, they cross the threshold carrying a lit '*soul candle.*' At a certain point during the rite, the candle is extinguished and then relit. This action symbolizes the change in the aspirant's condition: he or she came in as an outsider. The candle is put out, and once relit, the aspirant, now a member of the group, is bound by its rules and tradition. No one within the Craft can enforce belief; after all, how seriously these rules are taken is up to them.

We have all encountered people who join groups and then proceed to disrupt them, eventually departing and leaving behind them a troubled psychic atmosphere. Though when anyone relights their soul candle within this adoption rite, they must really and truly believe in the worth of what they do, and have full intention of keeping their oath - otherwise all the teaching enshrined in the concept of the Castle and the Goddess just:

"isn't worth a light"

and neither is their soul.

The
Stone
Stile

In 1993, Michael Howard's magazine, 'The Cauldron,' published an article that first had appeared in 'New Dimensions' in 1964, concerning one of Robert Cochrane's ritual workings, which was held in a cave in the Mendips. In yet another undated letter to William Gray, Cochrane also mentions an upcoming coven trip to the Llangastock caves in the Brecon Beacons, inviting Gray to join the group:

> "If you would really like to try your hand out, and incidentally work on top of a Welsh mountain the previous night with Jane and I, we will be setting out a fortnight from now and passing through Cheltenham about five o'clock on the Saturday."

He did not come however, which was just as well, for 'Aggy' was not an easy cave to deal with. In fact, for a witch who insisted on outdoor workings as much as possible, it seems almost contradictory that Cochrane should search for an accessible cave chamber big enough for magical workings; but he had good reason. He said that in the past, some of the old 'Clans' were made up of three Cuveens or groups each serving as custodians for one of three specific working sites that were additionally the focus of dedicatory rites specific to them.

In fact, these sites physically expressed within their topography, some part of the '**Faith**.' The Clan of Tubal Cain traditionally guarded its 'Three Rites' known as the 'Cave of the Cauldron,' the 'Chapel of the Grave,' and the 'Castle of the Four Winds'. Cochrane aimed to re-create the whole system in order to retrieve particular ancient mysteries from the past intrinsic to them. Thus, in the early years, he sought a cave in which to practice the mysteries of the Cauldron; within a reasonable distance from that cave there needed to be a ruined barn which could be made to resemble a ruined chapel, housing an open grave. The third site consisted of a plateau crowned Mound upon which to plot the topography of the Castle and its rings.[42]

If this seems like an ambitious project, consider that during those rebellious Sixties, old taboos were being swept away, including those within and against the Craft. The fact that Cochrane and those of us who were with him at the time did not fully accomplish this project in his time does not take away the fact that it was a conceptually sound idea within the Craft. Had we accomplished it then, perhaps today the Craft's image would be different. Cochrane habitually played his cards close to his chest, dropping interesting hints without actually revealing too much; such that one could never be sure if the hints came from a half-remembered tradition or his own creative imagination. Some of us know however, that in Oxfordshire, there is a ruined chapel housing an open grave that is sometimes used for a ritual connected to the *Rose beyond the Grave.*

Likewise, we'd heard quite separately from another old witch who had been a member of the **Faith** for a long, long time that his people once worked certain rituals in a cave, but then lost the use of it when the property it was on changed hands. He was a proper old countryman whose magical tradition was geared more towards the field and farm than the urban Wicca many had become accustomed to by that time. Born near the Cambridge/Hertfordshire boundary, he claimed that the old following drew its support from both sides of the county line. Alas, it is more or less all gone now; families had split up and moved away, just as he had done. The once close-knit village communities of the past ceased to exist in the same way; a loss that robbed the Craft of so much of its old traditions.

Apart from the rather general use of a cave to symbolize the 'Womb' like entrance to the Great Earth Mother, there is the afore-mentioned Anglo-Saxon tradition regarding three 'Wyrd' sisters, or Fates, who, despite Shakespeare's placement of them upon the open heath, make their home within a Cave around their Cauldron. Whether or not Shakespeare knew his witchcraft, he certainly knew his folklore. Not only do the three sisters spin the thread of a person's fate (or 'doom,' to use the Anglo-Saxon word) and then end it by cutting the thread, but they often did so around a cauldron. We see this cauldron as the magical vessel where past, present and future seethe in a state of flux and movement, symbolically becoming the place of rest for the soul awaiting rebirth. When Wyrd, or Fate, wills it, the soul leaves the cauldron and the sisters weave again the thread of that person's life into the fabric of existence, only to cut it in time, so that the soul returns to the place of rest.

In the Icelandic tradition we discover three sisters known as the *Urdr* (Fates) who tend the great World Ash Tree, Yggdrasil and axial post around which three worlds hang. Similarly, the Norse and Anglo-Saxon Pagan traditions adopted similar philosophies. From Raphael Hollingshead's *Chronicles of England, Scotland, and Ireland* published in 1578, we can see that William Shakespeare repeatedly consulted it for inspirational plots for his numerous historical plays, such that Macbeth met his witches not on the *"blasted heath"* but in the shadow of a tree, as the woodcut in the book reveals. We accept the three hags within the play as being the Fates and the tree as Yggdrasil, nourished with sacred water from their cauldron. If these sisters negate this 'Sisyphus' task, the sacred World Tree that spans the cosmos between the Underworld, through our own world ('Middle Earth') up to the heavens, will die along with these planes of existence. Then the state of flux within the Cauldron shall cease and past, present, and future will cease to exist - even the gods themselves will perish.

Wonderful, you say, a fine piece of mythology! What good is it? Before his death, Robert Cochrane spoke more than once of breaking with the past and moving on in what he called his personal *"magical argosy."* Had he lived, there is no doubt he would have fully enfleshed the scant forms he knew regarding the rites of the 'Cave of the Cauldron,' the 'Chapel of the Grave,' 'The Castle of the Four Winds' and the 'Stone Stile.' Today, the Clan of Tubal Cain continues this work. It is not that we literally believe that somewhere in this world the 'Wyrd' sisters are watering the World Tree; but we include that story here to show that at specific times we use caves for our workings not just: *"because that's the way it's done,"* but because our ancestors indeed had a tradition of a 'Sacred Cave' with its 'Cauldron' set within our mythos. As the following ritual demonstrates, when taking something from the Cauldron, you can in your mind's eye, link that action to the mythos behind and central to it.

The Stile:

For twenty years after Robert Cochrane's death in 1966, Bill Gray and I climbed Newtimber Hill every summer to the oak tree where we had first cast our circle to commemorate his passing, each carrying two small stones. The first thing we did upon reaching the site was to place those stones upon the existing 'cairn' formed over the years during our visits there. Our idea was to form a miniature 'Royal' Cairn as his memorial with a stone threshold for access to it. After crossing the 'stile,' which in this case was a small stone set in the ground to symbolize a full stile, we would then go to *the oak tree* that we had all worked beneath in years past. Once there we would light a candle and pour a libation to those times and to absent friends. Next we moved over to a small clump of holly where Bill [Gray] would leave a small token tied to a branch in remembrance of Cochrane.

Our final stop was the stump of an old oak, which served as the table for our token meal where we finished off the wine after pouring a final libation to the elemental spirits of the place. This very simple memorial rite demonstrates how easily sacred space is created even when that area is not necessarily a live working circle, but is perhaps more of a sacred area that includes a 'working' area. Certain trees, stones, hedges or other natural objects act as natural markers, and will serve to delineate the space, separating it visually and psychically creating a hypothetical line across the landscape so that your enclosure may be termed *'terra sanctus.'*

Interestingly enough, we have found that when people lay out their first 'compass' in a quiet and private place, then use it for few more rituals, the immediate area gradually takes on a life of its own, expanding until it becomes a sacred enclosure in the proper sense. This larger area offers space for such rituals as *'The Great Rite of Purification,'* or for the *'Rose Beyond the Grave,'* (if you do not have access to a ruined building), or even the spiral path to the mystic tower found in the Raven working of the shamanistic rites of the Clan (outlined in *Sacred mask, Sacred Dance.)*

The twin circles for 'All Hallow's Eve' may also be worked successfully in this space. Archaeological investigations of ancient pagan temples and shrines suggest similar natural growth patterns, forming a single focal point within the landscape features. Furthermore, perhaps our consistent memorial ritual in honour of Robert Cochrane repeated another ancient pattern whence a place associated with a particular person becomes a hallowed place of worship and a shrine to their memory. In the case of Newtimber Hill however, we decided that after twenty years it was finally time to let the site go and the memory fade. Having served its purpose, there was no further need for it; after all, only 'She' is eternal. Once or twice only have I felt the need to introduce anyone to this once scared area, to allow them to feel Cochrane's echo.

Consider this: When you locate your sacred enclosure on the crest of a hill among a few scattered trees, you are really taking the '**Faith**' back to where it started. When you continually work indoors, you lose touch with the spirit of nature which is the very foundation stone upon which the **Faith** was built. Even working in someone's yard or garden is not really quite the same thing; it is usually far too tame, neat, and tidy, something that nature definitely is not. When you work outdoors, you work among nature's visible cycles, feeling them in a way that a mere calendar-based ritual cannot compare to.

February, the close of one vegetative year and the start of another, with its empty fields and bare trees alerts the keen eye to the signs of new life. May's Eve arrives and those same trees are now garlanded with leaves and blossom, mirroring the tides of life, flowing strong and sure. Lammas is the time of plenty when the harvest ripens, yet in the very air we feel the ebbing flow of life. Hallowe'en, the time of the dead, when the circle under the oak is covered with fallen leaves (which should never ever be swept away), for dead though they are, beneath their cover the promise of life resides, which in turn serves the wellbeing of the soil upon which stands the sacred oak itself. Yes, the **Faith** is rooted in 'Nature' as well as in the interplay between the natural and the supernatural. So by working our magic where the deadening hand of the urban dweller has only lightly touched, we are linking up with the spiritual genius from whence the Craft first sprung.

9

The Rite of the Cave and Cauldron

D rawing upon the oracular symbolism of the Three Sisters of the Wyrd, this ritual falls firmly within the domain of the feminine subset of the Priestly mysteries.[43] Male cuveeners are present only as the *'congregation'* with the exception of the Magister whom we may here call the 'Divil.' This is the name he carried under the *'Old Covenant'* and the one recorded in the witch trials.

This Ritual of the Cave is divinatory in nature and is intended to give hints and some foresight into the coming year. The more one moves away from the more general Cuveen workings and their mysteries into the deeper mystical side of the Old **Faith**, the more important divination becomes, especially where it concerns the *'Rose Beyond the Grave'* (see forthcoming chapter) and other rites. Remember these are neither the lunar Cuveen workings nor the nine knots of the compass. Instead, they are performed separately from all normal workings and then only by *experienced* members of the Clan who should be well-versed in their mythic and mystical foundations.[44]

This ritual is intended for use in an actual cave, so there are physical considerations. First, use the spot respectfully. A central fire will not only smoke up the cave and degrade the underground environment; it will asphyxiate all participants as well. Use candles instead. If possible, lay out the compass beforehand. Mark the perimeter of a circle with ten to fifteen small stones, choosing stones that are naturally white or that you have whitened. The circle's diameter is not important so long as the three women have room to move around the cauldron without falling over each other. Outside this inner circle there should be space within the total working area for others within the gathering to 'pace a Mill' around it. Lots must be drawn between all female members of the Cuveen including the Maid, for the three named roles to determine which of them will become the three Sisters. This ensures that even in this naming act, Fate chooses Her vessels of prophecy in accordance with Her own decree.

Assuming that all is made ready with the ring laid out, all other members should stand outside the circle, allowing the Three Sisters of Wyrd to process into it. The first Sister carries the Cuveen sword, the second carries the cup and a small cauldron or bowl which she will place in the centre with the cup along side it. The third priestess carries a large flagon of spring water to pour into the cauldron and a ladle to be placed beside it on the opposite side from the cup. Then the Magister makes his address and Challenge as the 'Divil':

Divil: "Who are't thou? Who stand ye for? By what right are ye here?"

First Sister Of Wyrd: "We three represent the daughters of the Goddess Night, born of the sacred union of the Sun King and Moon Queen, mated in the deepest of silence according to the Testament of the Old Covenant."

Divil: "Name ye then the three daughters of the Goddess Night whom ye claim to represent."

First Sister: "I represent Wyrd, one of the three sisters who keep the cauldron."

Second Sister: "I represent Weorthend, one of the three sisters who keep the cauldron."

Third Sister: "I represent Skuld, one of the three sisters who keep the cauldron."

Three Priestesses [In Unison]: "In the name of the Goddess Night and her three daughters, we claim the right to serve the cauldron: one to stir, one to see, and one to tend it, as the Fates decree."

Divil: "In the name of all who are present, I challenge not thy right to do so. In the name of the Fates, let thy work be done."

The first sister steps close to the cauldron and with the sword's point she begins to stir the water while declaring:

"By joining sword to water, I re-create the union between the Sun King and Moon Queen in symbolic form, which once in the past gave birth to all events and things that have been, all events and things that are of the present and all events and things that have yet to come. For from within the never-ending movement of the Cauldron springs all creation; were it to cease, in its stillness lies death and the end to all such things. In its swirlings are generated the primal khaos charging the water therein with the very spirit and essence of life."

Taking the sword out of the pot, she hallows the cardinal points by flicking a few drops of water from its point while facing north, then east, followed by south and west. She then moves silently aside to allow the second priestess to approach the Cauldron. Kneeling down, the priestess acting as Seer focuses the whole of her attention on the water until her instinct tells her the time is right for her sisters to begin the slow rhythmic chant - the incantation to sing the Seeress into trance. Once she casts down her eyes, the 'Divil' leads the gathering in a slow, widdershins Mill.

This Mill is paced until the Seeress gets to her feet, no matter how long it takes for her to catch something of their 'Wyrd' from within the Cauldron.[45] Once the Seeress returns from her trance, the widdershins Mill must slowly grind to a halt. Again, in silence she takes up the cup which serves as a signal for the third Sister to approach the Cauldron and take up the ladle, filling it with water from the Cauldron. She then replaces the ladle within the Cauldron, and turns to face the cave entrance. Holding the cup in both hands, she raises it above her head invoking an inspirational blessing, beseeching wisdom to all true seekers bound in troth within the Covenant.

Lowering her cup, she takes a sip before offering it first to her Sisters and then to the 'Divil' and finally to all present. If the cup is emptied before everyone has drunk, she refills it without ceremony. Any water remaining in the cup when all have partaken of its contents, is returned to the Cauldron. With this, the Rite of the Cave is finished. A final blessing is given by the Maid, whichever Sister she has been fated to be for this rite. Again, its form is inspirational, being relevant to that time and place.

The gathering should then leave the cave with the Seeress carrying out the cauldron, being very careful not to spill any water. Once outside the cave it must all be poured into a bottle. The magically charged water it is simply too valuable just to tip out on the ground; rather it should be used as a lustration for cleansing the site chosen in preparation for the rite of the 'Rose beyond the Grave,' the 'Castle of the Four Winds' and possibly even the next 'Rite of the Stone Stile.' It should always be used for the 'Great Rite of Purification.'

Finally, all participants should gather in a quiet place for a feast, even if it is a token one. Do this as close as possible to the ritual site and outside rather than in. If the open air is good enough for any ritual, then it should be good enough for the feast afterwards.

To end on a personal note: when I first decided to record this ritual after several years of working it, I was forced to submerge myself in Anglo-Saxon mythology. To my surprise, every time I used the words 'Sun King' and 'Moon Queen' in my written notes, I found myself writing 'Sun Queen' and 'Moon King,' which was of course exactly how those heavenly bodies were reflected within their grammar. Having to correct myself more than once at least confirmed to me that I had tuned in better than I had imagined! Perhaps this is why the Rite of the Cave and Cauldron tends to shock and surprise people when they first work it. Performed properly and with full focus and intent, it does have a tendency to *run you* rather than you running it, despite its apparent simplicity.

As Robert Cochrane would have said:

"It's turning the clock back with a vengeance my friend, to become a time when anything can happen."

10
The
Castle
of the
Four Winds
(Castle Perilous)

When Robert Cochrane described the 'Rite of the Castle' in one of his letters to Bill Gray, he mentioned only the bare bones of the ritual; having all the requisite keys it enabled us to complete and work the rite to great effect and startling success. We quote that letter here because it conveys his essential spirit encapsulated within this rite more perhaps than others – it conveys something of his time and the memories of it. Most of all, it shows how the mythos of the Clan of Tubal Cain could be transmitted through ritual, which is all that we ask of any mystery Tradition. The following paragraphs are quoted from the letter:

> "This is purely a religious exercise, based upon an exceedingly ancient myth. It has to do with the structure and creation of the Ring. Like all witch religion, magic comes into it very strongly and it can be adapted for all purposes. With a slight alteration, it can become a purely magical symbol. Altered again, and it is the Gateway or Malkuth to the mysteries of the Craft."

Next, concerning the three concentric circles, Cochrane comments:

"As such, I am dealing with its most basic format."

He suggests that they would be made with materials such as follows:

The River: (1) Water and wine, vinegar and salt.

Death: (2) Willow for mourning. Birch for birth.

From the end to the beginning, back to the end.

The ash from these woods is usually used.

Life: (3) Man's labour and his work. Salt

"The centre is Avalon or to use the popular concept, Arianrhod's
Castle. The centre is the Inner Plane of Kabbalism and the ring is
altered to the purpose of the ritual so that it adapts to whatever
form the energy invoked takes, but still remains within the Castle. It
is basically four-sided, representing the elements in their original
form of the winds. Again it becomes eight-aspected in the symbol
of the white horse. Now around the Castle winds the River or Time.
It is this that distinguishes us [witches] from the 'quick and the
dead.' I suppose this [river] is classically the 'Lethe.' It is also the
beginning of power and [the] distinguishing mark between a witch
and a pagan, since a witch [re]crosses the river and a pagan remains
with the quick."[46]

The ash ring: This represents death or the state that all must enter
into to cross the river. It is also the symbol of sacrifice. It is comprised
of the ash of two woods and has a distinct philosophy of its own.

Salt: It is the ring of life and fire. It represents the illusory flesh and
the bitterness of life as well as its necessity.

"That comprises the basic format of the ring. Like all witch symbols it leads to many other things. I leave these answers to your intuition. In the ring the witch paces widdershins, never deosil. This is in honour of the triple Hekate, the Goddess of Life, Death and Wisdom who is Queen of the Castle. It is also correct psychically."

For the implements you will need:

'Knife.' This is the masculine tree. It represents intellect, Will, and represents the actual search for wisdom, experience and knowledge. It is also Choice, Love physical and generosity, Victory and conflict. Also Courage.

To that we add that the knife physically expresses the owner's soul, because at its dedication, part of the owner's personality and identity is instilled into the blade at the same time that it is magically charged. So when Cochrane ascribed these various qualities to the knife, they must also concern the soul and all the things we search for in this life.

'The Noose.' This is the feminine tree and should have five and three knots with a noose at one end. Traditionally, it should also be comprised of many materials, but hemp will do. The five knots are the round of life. The three knots are the Moon triad. It represents the feminine aspects of the knife, among other things.

In terms of the mythos, the five knots represent the 'round of life' or the five points of the pentagram where they also symbolize the five stages of development in a person's life. Those are birth, youth, maturity, old age, and finally death as the threshold towards eventual rebirth. The noose is the traditional sign of subjugation to Hekate as the End and Beginning of life, umbilical and a hangman's noose in one. It has many magical uses, most of which will come with intuition. One part of its use is to induce intuition by hanging: obvious reason, to overcome the flesh à la Tantrics. This mystical experience was also induced by its use for self-flagellation by some of the more mystical witches.

> 'Staff /Stang.' The Horse. It is the supreme implement. It represents the middle pillar Yggdrasill, the Ash at one end, the Rowan at the other. Its roots are Malkuth or the Gateway, that is physical experience, and at its top is the highest mystical experience. It should be forked at the top and bound at its base with iron. It is called the Gateway because it is phallic and presents Hermes the Guide, the Moon because it is the path to the mysteries, the foundation of wisdom and spiritual experience. It is Love because it is Beauty, the child of Wisdom (Horn Child). It is Death, the final transformation. In other words it is the single path of enlightenment.

The Stang in our tradition equates with the 'World Tree' of archaic shamanism exampled around the world, as well as the Middle Pillar of the Kabbalists. It spans the range of spiritual existence from the Underworld to that of our own ('Middle Earth') and beyond to the world of 'enlightened souls,' which is in fact the symbolic 'Castle' of the all-embracing primal spirit. Associations include the Greek God Hermes, who as guide between the worlds was manifest within the erect phallus and in the 'herm' posts strewn along the track-ways, marking boundaries for travellers and pilgrims.

The horns of the Stang signify the thighs of the 'Mother' ripe with Child; thus the stave itself becomes the umbilical cord linking the Earth Mother and the Old Horned God through Her son, the Young Horn King. Thus it is love, the union between male and female, attraction and counter-attraction that together generate beauty, the child of wisdom. To love is to find beauty, the art of giving, the joy of taking and above all, the pleasure of sharing. In an esoteric sense, the Stang also represents the Moon, symbol of the lunar mysteries, because by knowing, loving,

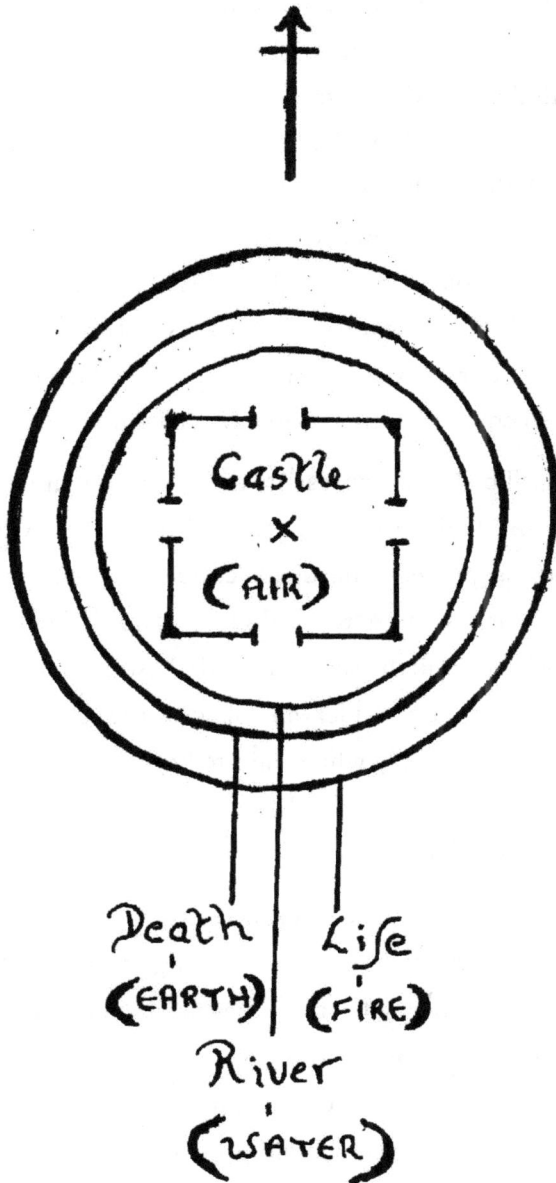

CAER SIDI CASTLE OF THE FOUR WINDS

and worshiping the Goddess as the foundation of all spiritual experience and wisdom, you can find the path of soul self-enlightenment that reaches far beyond the materialism of this world.

Finally, the Stang is death, the ultimate transformation where the questions posed by all religions find at last their answers. Although many are convinced of the soul's survival, most traditional witches subscribe to the concept of reincarnation and probe deep into our innermost being to discover traces of our past lives. Having said this, remember that we must all face death alone, whether it leads to nothing or to a spiritual existence beyond the grave. We of Tubal Cain believe the oft-re-incarnated soul will return eventually to the Source of all being.

> 'The Cloak.' The Cloak represents the concealment of the mystery and Night the Hider of Light. Also Humility and Charity which equals magical power. The cloak conceals us both literally and mystically. Worn in the circle it hides outward signs of rank and status. As all cats look the same in the dark, so should witches in the circle, so that to the outsider, all will look the same. There are no crowns in the Clan; only when the rite begins will the functions of the Maid, the Magister and other Officers be revealed. Thus the cloak also stands for humility.

In its mystic attributes the cloak represents the Goddess Night who cloaks the heavens with darkness, leaving only the tiny light from the witches' fire to show where Her mysteries are being worked. Through working the Castle and kindred rites, we learn Her secrets under the cloak of darkness. It is not the Clan's way to advertise ourselves with outward signs, with visible ornamentation; for we know that we stand before the gods who see beneath the cloak.

Now let us examine this letter's teachings sequentially. We have already described the Castle in its mythic form. In both ritual and its underlying mythos a pathway to the Castle is described. Like the Mandalas of Tibetan Buddhism the ritual creates a sort of schematic diagram of what truly are indescribable states of being. Because of its symbolic connection with the altering of consciousness, the ritual uses a spiral path rather than a linear path, suggesting the spiral journey within.[47]

In many ways the philosophy of the Castle Perilous is very similar to the one illustrated within the mythos, as both represent a pathway to the Castle of the Pale-Faced Goddess. However, that other is a map through the Underworld, whereas this rite offers a magical way of reaching the Four Square Castle of the Winds and so is not quite the same thing. The *Source* of all magical power is to be found at its centre.

Hence when you hear witches saying: *"the four becomes eight,"* it means that what is done in this world is repeated in the psychic world. If the Castle was a physical building, as you walked around the outside, you would see four walls. Then, if you were to walk around the inside, you would see four more walls – the inverse sides in fact. Yet how many of us have seen *both* sides of the wall at the same time? How many have seen the intersection between the physical and the spiritual symbolized by the white horse, the steed of spiritual freedom?

The outermost ring or moat, representing human labour, is formed using salt. Strange though it may seem in an age when people are often encouraged to use less salt in their diet than before, salt equates with life and work. Yet salt is necessary to human life, and its importance sticks in our language: the word 'salary,' from the Latin word for salt is one example. Another is the saying: *"He isn't worth his salt,"* meaning he is worthless and not earning his salary. At one time much of our food, be it meat, fish, vegetables, even pickles could only be preserved through salting until electricity made refrigeration possible; salt then was an invaluable process. Since salt is primarily sourced inland and was once dug from the Earth (at sites such as Salzberg – 'Salt Mountain' in Austria), it has long been associated in magic with the Earth, through the 'sweat' endured in the simple toil of existence. Thus, by making the outer circle of salt, we consecrate our efforts to the Divine Creatrix.

The second ring is formed by the ashes of two woods, traditionally birch and willow. Willow has long associations with sorrow and mourning while birch has associations with rebirth. Together, they stand for the cycle of death (which is mourned) and rebirth (which may also be mourned since it leads only on towards death). All we can leave from this cycle is something to mark our passing, something to be remembered by, but all earthly power and glory are transient at best. In the literal sense, what we leave behind are only mouldering bones or ashes; only the immortal soul knows the reality of existence on both sides of the grave. After death, we seek to cross the river, here symbolized by a mixture of water, wine, vinegar, and salt. Here all memories of earthly life are washed away from the soul. The wine represents the good things of life, all of our joys. But the vinegar represents life sorrows, its bitterness, its disappointments. The salt, as above, represents life's work, and the water cleanses and heals the soul that passes through it.

'Crossing the River' leads us to one of Cochrane's more enigmatic afore-mentioned teachings, which is the distinction he draws in his letter between 'witch and Pagan.' In the years since his death, Pagan, usually written with a capital P to distinguish it from the other meaning of: 'an irreligious person,' has become a self-description for many people who also call themselves witches. We often read that:

"witches are Pagans but not all Pagans are witches."

This means simply that the term 'Pagan' is more inclusive. But for Cochrane, the witch was someone who had deliberately and consciously chosen to tread this spiral path and prepare him/herself *in life* for a separate afterlife. Cochrane's teaching of the Craft, in common with others, included the idea that eventually the soul will reach a state of spiritual awareness such that it no longer needs to manifest itself in a physical body, instead returning to the Source from whence it came.

We say that the individual soul gains a little more spiritual awareness, understanding, and knowledge with each rebirth. Logically, it stands to reason that at some point in these rebirths, certain souls will find themselves standing at the metaphoric crossroads. Some people claim that witches are born and cannot be 'made.' Perhaps we can reconcile those two attitudes with the thought that joining a Cuveen means submitting yourself to the will of Hekate in preparation for the end and beginning of all things. It is She and none other whom will claim Her own; and each of us that hears Her call has the choice to respond or not. Should you respond to the call of 'blood to blood,' you have begun to understand the true meaning of 'Fate.' You alone, from that point, become responsible for everything you do - you cannot ask anyone else for absolution. Fate as the Pale-Faced Goddess has ordained that you must carry your deeds yourself and answer for them at some future time.

The Castle, a Ritual of Self-Discovery:

The Castle is more a ritual of self-discovery than a group working. The person working it opens himself or herself up to the forces that are commonly termed: 'The Old Ones'. By tradition, the witch works alone on this occasion, although if the bond between members is strong and intimate, then up to a maximum of four may attempt it together. But no more than this; why this is so, should become clear as we move on to discuss the rite itself.

This rite is best suited like many of the Clan's rituals to outdoor working. If for whatever reason this proves impossible then certain adaptations and allowances will need to be made for working indoors.

The Clan of Tubal Cain maintains a long tradition of cave and hilltop ritual sites. Given this predilection we travel light: some salt, a small bag of wood ash from burnt willow and birch twigs, plus a small plastic bottle filled with a 50/50 mixture of water, wine, vinegar, and salt. A cloak, knife, magnetic compass, and personal stang/staff will also be required. Light is provided by four candles in wind-proof jars or candle lanterns.

Unlike the standard working where the compass is set down upon the working area with a 'gate' or 'bridge' to enter and leave by, the Castle Mandala or 'circle' has none. Instead, each ring or 'moat' is laid from *inside* its boundary without breach. The candles are placed at the four cardinal points and lit last of all. Those undertaking this journey will tread the spiral pathway on the symbolic journey through life into death and beyond as they cross the river of forgetfulness to the 'Spinning Castle of the Pale-Faced Goddess.' Likewise, upon withdrawal from the Castle, the return journey re-establishes the conscious mind within the manifest plane, hopefully the richer for it, be that in terms of 'power' or knowledge gained from working the mystery of the Castle.

Strangely enough, for so formal a rite, it is deceptively simple to execute, requiring very little in the way of complicated chanting or calling on the Old gods. To begin, each person taking part must place their stangs/staffs in the absolute centre of the circle. Either the Magister or one person only should be elected to lay the rings as the others follow them around, making the 'shift' between the realms as they step back through each ring towards the centre from the outer most circle, the circle of salt, life and manifestation. The words used when laying the rings, may be as simple as the following example:

"With this salt, which represents my labours and the work, I set the ring of life to the plane of earth."

Begin at the northern marker and lay a full circle of salt from the

116

container, making sure that you stay inside it. This is the *Ring of Life*. All step back from it.

The next ring to be set is the *Ring of Death*, usually spaced about ten to twelve inches in from the salt circle:

> "With the ashes of willow and birch, signifying the mourning of death and rebirth from its icy thrall, I separate myself from the Ring of Life, just as death severs the flow of life. Thus from the end to the beginning and back to the end shall time and experience run their course. Here I set the Ring of Death to the plane of the heavens."

Starting again in the north, lay the circle of ash. All step back. Move towards the centre about ten to twelve inches again to lay the final ring, of the Lethe itself. Pour the wine and vinegar mix, full circle:

> "Thus the River of Forgetfulness has separated me from the plane of death and the effects of death itself, for I have advanced beyond the place of the 'quick and the dead' to stand upon the threshold of the Void. I have trodden the path in spirit before, now purposefully, I do so in the flesh. Finally I set the Ring of Time within the eternal cosmos (Ceugent)."

Next light four candles beginning in the north, placing one at each compass point in the following order: north, south, east, west, marking the four cardinal gateways of the compass. To reinforce the psychic image of the Four-Square Castle, place white-painted stones or poles at each cardinal point. Finally, all of those present (if the rite is not performed solo) gather around the central Stang, which has now become the *axis mundi* denoting the point linked to the Source whence all power springs.[48]

The Magister must activate the compass by summoning the Winds, primarily at each cardinal point in turn.[49] Those working this rite must at this point devise by inspiration some method of connection at least to the winds. Traditionally, the art of 'whistling down the winds' is one that is passed between mentor and student, from Master to aspirant. It cannot be transmitted by words upon paper. How to work the 'keys' or tools (Knife, the Noose, the Stang, and Cloak) during this rite is for each individual to decide. Some prefer silent contemplation while others may prefer a chant. It is imperative that each tool is recognized as a major 'key' before this rite is even attempted. This may require some study and considerable meditation.[50] A simple set of invocations could begin like this:

"I call on the Knife, male in essence, intellect, will, and the search for wisdom, experience and knowledge."

Think very carefully about what these words mean. Allow the mind to become blank so that it may begin unconsciously, the process of redefining the meaning of the knife and the terms previously related to it: intellect, will, wisdom, and knowledge. Likewise, treat the Noose in the same way, paying special attention to the meanings of the five and three knots, the round of life. Move onto the Stang and the Cloak to conclude their allusive significances. Pause in contemplation of the purpose of this rite. When all meditations are finished, douse the candles, simply gather everything together silently and, move southwards (life) directly across all three rings. Focus on re-crossing the river, returning through death to life and the world that you symbolically left behind at the beginning of the rite. The 'Castle of the Four Winds' may sound simple enough, but because it induces such a profound and inexpressible experience for each individual, it can help illuminate the pathway to the 'Spinning Castle,' bringing comprehension of its reality and true purpose.

11
The
Rose
Beyond
the
Grave

Through these rites: *'The Stone Stile;' 'The Cave of the Cauldron;'* and *'The Castle of the Four Winds,'* we complete what we earlier described as a unique aspect of the Tubal Cain tradition in this concluding rite named - *'The Rose Beyond the Grave.'* Its concentration and primary focus on the preparation for the afterlife leads onto an eventual rebirth among like souls. Rooted in ancient shamanic experience, its mythos was later developed significantly by Robert Cochrane, to form the core of our particular branch of Traditional Witchcraft. Once this is realised, others choosing to follow these guidelines can organize and operate these rituals in their own right.

The 'Rose Beyond the Grave' carries at least two levels of symbolic meaning. The first it shares with the broader occult tradition where the rose represents secrecy in those things which are not discussed with outsiders. The second level is more particular to Traditional Witchcraft. The origin of the rose as a symbol of secrecy may be traced with some degree of certainty to pagan Roman times, supposedly when Cupid is said to have given a rose to Harpocrates the God of silence, to signify the concealment of the secrets of Venus. Hence early Christians rejected the rose as a decorative motif because of this association with Roman depravity. Yet the rose reasserted itself, as testified in sacred art and architecture especially during the high gothic and Romanesque periods of medieval history.

As an aside, the humble rose hip was an inexpensive and ideally shaped material for making rosary beads - reinforcing its name, which allegedly stems from the Virgin Mary's allegorical 'crown of roses.'[51] Today, in the legal and political worlds, trials and proceedings that are 'sub rosa,' or 'under the rose' are those held discreetly behind closed doors in select conclaves. Among occultists, the rose thus symbolizes the 'hidden aspects' of the mysteries. Perhaps borrowing from the legal profession, occultists began to use the symbol of the rose as a means of saying that some

teachings are discussed discerningly, shared only among those elected individuals deemed to be trustworthy. In some (not all) cases being passed only under a pledge of silence. In the case of the 'Clan of Tubal Cain,' it is also associated with the grave. We picture the rose lying at the bottom of an open grave signifying our belief that there is something more than just a sharp, sudden end to life, a promise of something 'other' yet to be revealed, which will be found in the experiences beyond death and the grave.

Still, no one as yet has offered concrete and irrefutable proof of life after death that would stand up in a court of law. No matter what our religious beliefs may be and no matter how much we delve into our innermost being to dredge up past-life experiences, in the end all that we have left is our *personal* belief in the existence of a soul and of a life beyond the grave. Only when we cross from life to death can we find the true answer to the secret of: 'The Rose Beyond the Grave.' If we believe in the existence of an immortal soul, we are faced with the question of what happens to it after death. Since every religion offers its own version of the afterlife, they cannot all be right. Or can they? We are told:

"For many eons the human spirit had no abode; then finally by desire to survive [it] created the pathway into the Other-worlds. Nothing is got by doing nothing, and whatever we do now creates the world in which we exist tomorrow. The same applies to death: what we have created in thought, we create in that other reality. We should remember that Desire was the first of all created things."

If this is an inspired explanation of truth, then there can be as many Otherworld places of the dead as there are religions, and each one will be equally valid in its own right without denying or contradicting the validity of others created by the collective minds and desires of a religion's followers. Because we enforce a belief in re-incarnation, it therefore exists, because we have used our divinely given gifts to create our own existence within those parameters of eternity.

Try the following visualization, keeping in your mind that we picture the soul's journey through the Underworld as crossing a river, then facing desolate wastelands, which with the aid of a miracle begin to bloom as the soul passes through them. When we picture the wastelands blooming, the flower we see is the blood-red 'Rosa gallica' (French rose), the same rose placed at the bottom of the open grave.

Close your eyes for a few moments after you read the next paragraph and recreate it as vividly as you can.

"After the ferryman has brought you across the river to the edge of the Otherworld, he leaves you standing on its further bank. There in front of you is a desolate plain covered by gnarled and stunted bushes, stretching as far as the eye can see. A Castle stands in the distance, perched on a rocky outcrop. As you begin to walk along the path threading its way across this barren landscape, the thorny bushes on either side of the path start to burst into life, first budding, then flowering. With gathering speed, more and more bushes burst into life as you walk along. By the end of your walk, the whole landscape is abloom – a rich carpet of blood-red flowers that encircle the Castle which rises imposingly above them."

The traditional designs of 'Castles and Roses' sometimes seen in folk-art decoration carry this theme, interpreted by Traditional witches as follows: The rose of secrecy laid at the bottom of a grave becomes transformed into the newly blooming bushes. Now it is the rose that blooms beyond the grave. With death, the secret of the grave is now revealed to the: 'passed over' soul, that go on to discover what we believe is hidden within the walls of the Spiral Castle of the Pale-Faced Goddess. So any depiction of the Castle surrounded by a garland of roses announces

Gateway

Chapel

Grave

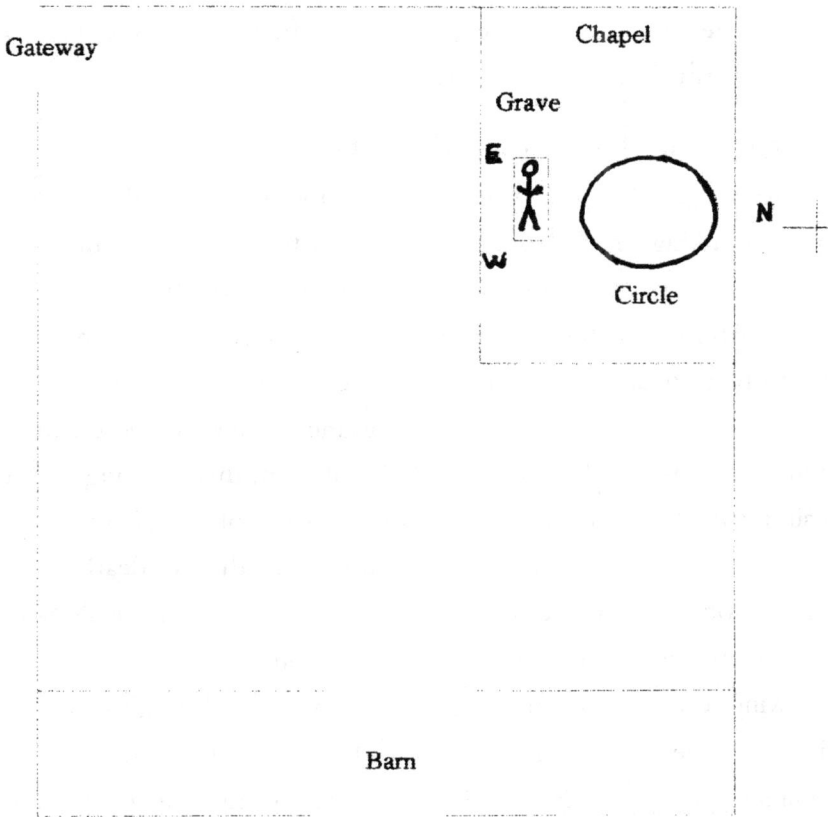

Circle

N

Based on the site used by the Oxfordshire group

and one that I've worked with them in the past.

Not drawn to scale.

Barn

ROSE BEYOND THE VEIL [AFTER JOHN]

to the pilgrim seeker that there are secrets to be discovered in the home of the Divine Creatrix. They are revealed to us first through the shamanic trance-state rituals and finally in death.[52]

The Ritual of the Chapel of the Grave:

When Robert Cochrane first revived and elaborated upon this ritual, he was not thinking of the usual Cuveen rites that celebrate life and its passages, but instead he chose to recognize death as the final transformation. Our tradition has a doctrine of re-incarnation, but in order to be re-incarnated, you must first die. Typically, many occultists will say that you are then reborn in circumstances that reflect your conduct in your previous life. To the Clan of Tubal Cain, this teaching seemed too simplistic, for it failed to answer the question of: 'why.' What is the point of living life after life, interspersed with death after death, for no better reason than to give us a choice between virtue and evil? Surely there must be more to it than this! But if the soul evolves from a state of unknowing to a state of knowing, it stores wisdom through many lives until it becomes one with the Godhead, symbolized by the inwardly spiralling circle that reaches back from where it came. The journey ends where it began. We have always found that when a person reaches a certain stage in their spiritual development, they find themselves asking three questions which only they can answer:

"Who am I?
What have I become?
Where am I going?"

Those who have undergone the ritual and lain within cold damp earth of an open grave say it does not mean they are now in a state of spiritual perfection, where re-incarnation is redundant. Rather it serves to remind them of its teachings, creating a meaningful illusion of the

124

experience that we will all one day face as a different reality. And who knows, some person, some night, will in a divinely-inspired vision catch a glimpse of the newborn child who will grow eventually into the beautiful young woman who, once stripped of all her finery will stand revealed as 'Naked truth,' thus replacing belief with certainty in that person's mind.

The 'chapel,' so called for its ruin, is an abandoned place of worship where ancient mysteries were once explored. Abandoned by its congregation, forgotten by the world, its altar stands bare. The lamp is unattended while the building itself has an atmosphere of neglect, damp, and decay tinged with desolation. Thus it remains until another gathering of seekers discover it and reawaken the old powers that haunt its walls by working their own particular rituals. By 'chapel' it is not inferred the ruined building must have served an ecclesiastical function. In Cochrane's day, the Cuveen searched for a derelict stone barn with an earthen floor and could not find one; since that time, others have been located. One group in Oxfordshire did however, gain access to an actual ruined church.

Whatever site you choose, the grave should be placed to the north of an east-west line drawn through the centre of the building. Leave enough room between the north wall and the grave that people can walk up and then step over the grave, which needs be no more than a foot to eighteen inches deep. If you are unable to find a ruined building to specifications, however, you may still carry out the ritual of the Chapel of the Grave in an open space with the walls symbolically marked. The grave is oriented to an east-west axis, as stated, for only the living may greet the rising Sun, while the souls of the dead 'go west:'[53]

"into the golden sunset ... into the golden rest."

Build a small fire to the south of the grave, so that all participants must cross the grave when moving from the North to reach the fire and the ritual area. When they do so, they ritually leave behind them all the trials and tribulations of life. They leave the Northern sector ruled by the Pale-Faced Goddess to enter the quarter of the 'Mother,' who resides in the South, protecting all lost souls seeking peace and comfort.

The ritual officers are chosen by lot, based on the premise that everyone taking part should be equal in knowledge and understanding. We place the selection in the hands of Blind Fate so that She chooses to whom She wishes to reveal Her mysteries, thus avoiding the old trap of placing too much power or bias in the hands of those who hold permanent office. No-one is excluded by gender, as both male and female participants take place in the drawing of lots, which should be held a few days before the ritual so that the two assistants or servitors will have time to prepare certain items.

One servitor prepares a brush used to sprinkle the 'charged water' saved from the ritual of the *'Cave and Cauldron.'* He or she should collect a bundle of twigs, binding them at one end with natural hemp twine to form a handle before trimming the unbound ends to an even length. Ideally, the brush should contain willow for mourning, birch for rebirth and ash for the Horned God. Assembled that way they read:

> "We recognize death and bewail its coming, but accept our rebirth and the recovery of our true selves. This is what the Old gods have placed upon us when they made us People of the **Faith**."

If you cannot easily obtain willow, birch, and ash, then use what grows locally, for the ability to improvize is essential. It is enough that the participants know what the brush of twigs stands for. The servitors and officers should bring the following items to the ritual site:

Lustration brush (as described above)

A small glass or metal bowl

A single red rose

A bottle of water saved from the 'Cave and Cauldron' rite

A bottle of red wine and the Cuveen chalice

Enough bread to give everyone attending a token piece

A little bag of salt wrapped up in a twist of paper

Wood for a small fire

If anyone feels more ambitious, they may wish to bake something more appropriate than bread for this rite; the tokens aptly named the 'beans of the dead are absolutely perfect.'[54] Assuming that the rite will begin just before the witching hour of midnight, the servitors should be on site no later than 11:30 p.m. having taken with them everything necessary for the rite itself. Their first job should be to build and light the fire, then fill and set out the bowl of water, together with a lustration brush, salt, and rose near the fire. If the rite begins about 11:45 p.m., then it will be well underway at midnight when the tides of time and life are at their lowest ebb.

Participants should gather on the Northern side of the grave, the Mound. First the servitors walk around the east end of the grave to the fire, where the water, lustration brush, salt, and rose are placed. One servitor takes the bowl of water another takes the rose, while the third takes up the lustration brush. All three move towards the near edge of the grave. The servitor with the bowl, kneeling, offers it to the person with the lustration brush. That person continues to lustrate and hallow both grave and the Northern sector where it resides by sprinkling water again making their invocation composed of a few simple, but succinct lines of inspirational poetry. These should 'spell' out the sanctification of the space in and around the grave. A simple example would be:

"With water from the Cauldron, I sanctify this grave, the hallowed symbol of the Royal Cairn, the empty mausoleum, and the liminal boundary between the world of the flesh and that of the spirit."

The servitor with the rose also bends their knee presenting it to the officiating officer as before, who then drops it in the open grave with the flower head pointing east, which denotes the 'head' of the grave. Another simple invocation is expressed, describing the journey about to be undertaken, the hopes for its journeymen and the needs for discretion concerning what they may witness there. Something along the lines of the following:

> "By placing the rose in the grave, we express both the mystery of death and that which lies beyond death even unto the final transformation. This grave, once crossed, seals the oath of silence and your pledge to never reveal what is experienced there to anyone beyond the Troth of the Covenant. Anyone unwilling to abide, should peacefully take their leave of this company of fellows. Those who stay, yet break this solemn pledge of the rose, shall be cast out body and soul from this communion of the faithful. To stay or leave all must declaim that intent:"

cuveenors add: "This we know and this we accept. In the name of the rose, so be it sworn."

One by one, each person must step across the open grave to form a circle around the fire. When all have crossed, the officiating officer should 'hallow' the three remaining quarters. Cochrane executed this in total silence. Should anyone attempting to re-create this rite feel the need for spoken words, then an appropriate invocation must be chosen for each direction. For example, the two servitors moving to the East, dedicate it to the Fiery Dawn and to the Son of the Morning Star; the officiating officer could sprinkle a few drops of charged water saying:

> "With this water, I hallow East, the dawn and light of the Morning Star."

This could be similarly repeated at the southern and western quarters accordingly, making pertinent substitutions, as follows below:

South, dedicated to the Grain Goddess of Life. Hers is the spirit to be chased round the field by the reapers until She becomes trapped in the last sheaf to be cut. She symbolizes the New that comes from the Old, and Her sector is hallowed with a few more drops of water sprinkled from the brush with the prayer of:

"With this water, I hallow South and the spirit of Madame la Guiden, the Pale Corn Goddess."

West is the section of the dread Old Man of the Sea, the Waters of the Lethe. The officiate sprinkles more water and makes this invocation, preferably silently:

"With this water, I hallow the waters of the Lethe."

Finally, he or she blesses the gathering with a few more drops of water together with a benediction expressed aloud:

"May She who stands before all things indescribable and incomprehensible through Her Grace and Charity fill us with the knowledge of Her ways and to fear not the life we have in this world, thus living it to the full. For what we do now will *shape our* coming lives. In the name of the All Mother of the mysteries of Life and Death, I give this blessing."[55]

Although the preparation as outlined above could be described as 'information' only, distinct as it is from any revelation regarding content, the actual experiences that form the purpose of this rite is as should be expected strictly 'sub-rosa' (under the rose-and still withheld). But Robert Cochrane himself touched on what occurred during one particular ritual working, within one of his letters to William Gray; although in discretion, he did not give further explanation nor reveal its original context:[56]

> "I woke up suddenly to find myself sitting upright in my own body, half in half out. A dark form was in the room with me, and I was genuinely frightened. Protesting weakly, I was hauled out of myself and taken to a wood, into the presence of my Master, seen for the first time. (He said) – 'Here She comes. Bend your knee to the Lass. Let us worship Her.' I looked up from the ground where I was lying (The moss was so distinct and so real that every individual plant stood out clearly in the most brilliant green) and I saw coming through the oak trees towards me a brilliant photism, the vision of Our Lady as an ageless beauty, naked and riding a horse, bathed in brilliant, pure light also. I have never felt anything like I did then before or since, but then I was shot back to myself with a thundering crash and got out of bed trembling and shaking."

Without revealing too much detail, what is seen here is Naked truth as the glorious Maid. We can freely say that events in the ritual of the 'Rose Beyond the Grave' tend to fall into a similar pattern. After the blessing, all participants should begin by treading a slow, widdershins Mill, and it is during this that the first of the phenomena should begin to manifest. First of all, the crying of a newborn baby will be heard, signifying the awakening of the Primal Spirit from the Great Silence, the Source and origin of all things spiritual. The 'Old Man' will make his visit next, and everyone will be aware of His unmistakeable presence. He is the messenger of the Goddess Herself, although He can take many forms. Cochrane gives a good description, even though the setting in the letter is wrong (subject to the rose again). He was dead right where he writes:

> 'I was hauled out of myself."

130

This is precisely what happens. You *are* hauled out of your body into the presence of the Master. There in the Otherworldly greenwoods, both you and He will give homage to this phenomenal Vision of truth. What Cochrane saw and described was identical to the experience of others who have worked this ritual; and you may likewise see Her too. Once you come crashing back into your body, shaking and trembling with a mixture of awe and fear, you will realize that everyone is still pacing the widdershins Mill and that none of you have stopped. This too seems to wind down naturally, leaving everyone feeling totally drained.

The ceremony ends with the dedication of the bread and wine or 'Houzle,' for which everyone faces cardinal West for dedication to the spirit of the Castle, the home of all those souls who have departed within the *Faith*, awaiting rebirth. If led by a man, and where neither servitor is female, then the priest must choose a lady from the gathering to assist in the preparation of the Houzle. Should the reverse occur, then she must choose her male helper from the ranks of the gathering. Even though this rite is beyond what might be thought of as the 'basic' Craft, we believe that only a man and woman working together can consecrate the bread and wine. This may take the following form, by example only:

Participants gather in a semi-circle around the eastern side of the fire facing West. The officiating couple should stand west of the fire, also facing Westwards. The female priest holds the bread on a platter while the male priest sprinkles it with a little salt, saying:

"Symbolizing man's labour, I dedicate this bread with salt to the Grace of Our Lady who is before all things, the eternal and everlasting Goddess. May She fill us from within, increasing the knowledge of Her and Her wisdom as we partake of this food in Her presence."

Putting the platter to one side, the female priest then holds out the cup for the officiating priest to fill. This done, she elevates the cup as he declaims:

"I dedicate this cup to our Lady and invoke the blessing of Her spirit and Grace to flow into this wine and thus to all who partake of Her cup, imbibed with Her Serene mystery."

The two of them then stand close together, and the lady once again raises the cup to a height where the priest can pass his arms around the outside of hers. Then, joining his hands on the hilt of the knife, he lowers its point into the wine. Taking up the platter of bread, he offers each person a piece, saying:

"In the name of 'Our Lady' eat, and share Her bounty."

The lady follows him with the cup, and when each person has eaten the bread, she offers them a sip of wine saying:

"Partake of 'Our Lady's' grace, supped here in Her presence."

Only when all have been served, the officiants may serve each other with the last of the bread and wine. Finally, the cup is refilled. Standing facing West, with the fire at her back, the lady pours a final libation to the 'Lady of the Castle,' declaring:

"To you Lady, as Suzerain of the Castle wherein one day our souls will find rest, we pour this final libation. We pour it for the shades of those of the Shadow Company, may they be reborn once again into the **Faith**, as may we all. Lady, by your Grace and Charity, may it be so."

The wine is slowly poured onto the ground before the cup is turned over fully. If she is one of the servitors or another member of the gathering, she must place the cup by the fire to signify that she has now reverted to her former status. But if, however, she is the presiding officer, she formally closes the rite by saying:

"The rite is finished, the libation poured, time calls us to leave this sacred place, but not before I call down a final benediction upon you all. May Our Lady and the Old Horned One serve and keep you. So Motte Ye."

To leave the circle, all participants must re-cross the grave in the North. The servitors stay behind to gather everything up and douse the fire. Traditionally, we hold the feast which follows this rite, a short distance away from the site, around a second fire which has been lit specially for the occasion.

Anyone reading this rite having intention to work it, is encouraged to change the wording to express what feels right for them. It is the pattern of the ritual after all that is important, not what is said. And what more can you want than that?

ROYAL ROSE

133

12
The
Great
Rite Of
Purification

Both Robert Cochrane and William G. Gray took an occultist's view of pop music; that is to say, they saw within it, various forms of evocation. In the same letter in which he gives Gray a riddle, Cochrane observes that attendees at rock concerts use magic unknowingly, raising what their ancestors called 'Cain' or the unbalanced forces of chaos.[57] In the mad sixties, when the Beatles were at their height of popularity, Cochrane writes:

> "All that noise, sexual hysteria and so on is a dangerous force to play with and this is what the Beatles are doing. I would not be surprised to read that (A) that a meeting of R&B had evolved into a fertility rite and (B) that one of the Beatles had come to a very bloody and untimely end, à la primitive magic as the God of Vegetation."

The letter was undated, but it had to have been written before Cochrane's own death in the summer of 1966. And of course John Lennon of the Beatles met a tragic death when shot by an enraged fan, though not until 1980. The strangest aspect with regard to Robert Cochrane's prophecies was that he delivered them without ceremony. While talking about something else he would quite effortlessly unfold a prediction that was accurate to the Nth degree. Yet his manner was such that you could not be sure if he was serious or not.

He made an extremely valid point in that letter with regard to the noise, sexual hysteria, and general atmosphere of a rock concert, in that we really do have all the elements present that go to make up what is popularly referred to as *'chaos magic'* where nature's elemental forces leak through into this world. What is often lacking though, is a practitioner skilled enough in chaos magic to be able to manipulate this potential. Yet there are those who deliberately follow the path of chaos, perhaps because both psyche and ego feed vampire-like, on the humiliation, misery, and suffering created amongst their followers, something a true *'witch/pellar/ member of the people'* would never do.

Even so, any magical group working closely together will, over time, build up what is often called a 'group soul' or Egregore that will develop to a life of its own. This is often to the good, and is in fact desired in most cases. However, those who plunge into repeated and frequent magical workings where the mood or purpose is heavy or unbalanced may find themselves engulfed in a rather heavy and oppressive psychic atmosphere, even when their actual goal was something as positive as healing. This is regrettably something that most 'how-to' books do not tell you, but it is nonetheless a fact.

We have for example, worked to cure someone's illness and subsequently found everything going wrong on a psychic level. It was like pushing through sludge to make any contact with the Other Side; yet after a ritual purification, everything changed for the better. Less frequently, events may appear to conspire against the group and the possibility of a curse laid at the door has to be considered. This is extremely rare I hasten to add; but it remains an unfortunate possibility. Eventually that curse will have to be lifted and sent back to where it came from.

Laying Out the Working Area:

First of all, the Magister must lay out a small circle, where the 'burdens' of the soul will be left behind. The exact dimensions are unimportant, so long as it is big enough for one person to move in and out without falling over one of the candle lamps in the process.

This circle is marked by four candles at the four cardinal points of the compass. In total silence, but with absolute focussed intent, a trail of salt is laid from north to east, around to the south and west and finishing up in the north, thus marking the boundary.

Next light the candles, dedicating each one to the guardian of that quarter. Beginning with the East candle, the form could be as follows:

EAST:

> "I dedicate the flame to the unseen spirit of this place, may its light draw you to me."

Repeat at the other three points. The one dedicating the 'circle' steps back declaring:

> "Whoever enters here must purge their fears, discarding those things that cause grief to the soul. Heavy burdens will fall away, into this ring of salt. Any curse shall remain within to be cleansed by the earth beneath. So be it done."

The next step depends on an ancient belief that iron can break an evil spell. Place a large iron bar about eighteen inches away from the southern candle lamp, outside the salt ring. This must be stepped upon as each person exits the ring, ensuring that they are earthed completely. Primitive though this may appear, time has hallowed it, and it works.

Outside the salt ring, build four small fires, in a diamond shape to represent the fiery furnace of purification and transformation, expressed by Hargrave-Jennings in his 1870 book *The Rosicrucians: Their Rites and Mysteries* as:

> "the self-same urn of the fiery transformation in which all things of the world change."

For ages fire has been considered to be the great purifier, and in the mystical sense, the spirit of the magician passes through the fire of purification where illusion is burnt away and his or her spirit is hardened and tempered by knowledge which produces the cutting edge of the will. The act of stepping into the centre of the four small fires symbolizes the sloughing away of psychic debris, the charnel flame turning all to dust.

The Stang is placed on the furthest point of the diamond, on the opposite point to the salt ring. To re-iterate, so far there is a salt ring, an iron bar, a fiery square and the Stang. Representing the Old Horned God it is left completely bare, sans arrows and garland. Nearer to the actual larger working area and fire place a pot of ritually charged water. Lay the compass last of all.

The Purification Ritual:

Each person opting to undertake this rite must (unless, as in rare cases, it becomes necessary for all) enter the salt ring alone, pausing awhile in each space, focusing hard with full will and intent, first upon the purge within the salt ring, then earthing upon the iron bar, followed by the sloughing within the square of fire. Whether it be through a sense of depression or something else, the power of a curse can take on a tangible form. This is the thing that has to be left behind, so when it is felt that it has been lifted, move onto the next stage, past the iron bar.

We have found it particularly effective if the person in the 'furnace' imagines being engulfed by fire, searing their flesh until they emerge phoenix-like flames, born anew. However you visualize the effects, you must pour your soul into them; otherwise, you might as well have stayed home and watched television.

Upon reaching the Stang, kneel before it, invoking by example, words such as these:

> "May the Horned One by prayer and supplication shield and guard me from my enemies. May He stand between me and the ills wished upon me by others. By right of the Covenant I claim protection in His name."

The final station for the purification is the pot or cauldron of 'charged' water (saved from the Cave and Cauldron Rite); in other words, water that has been ritually consecrated according to Clan Rites. These waters now represent the River Lethe, the Waters of Oblivion, which flows between this world and the next and is where the earthly past of every soul that crosses it is washed away. This meaning is reflected in our invocation at this point:

> "As I draw water from this Sacred Vessel of Our Lady, may it be as the 'Waters of Oblivion' - a soothing balm to body and soul; may these healing waters relieve all past hurt; may the memory of it fade into nothing. By right of the Covenant I claim succour in Her name."

Finally, the participant crosses the besom into the working ring. When all are assembled there, the Magister moves over to the salt ring announcing:

Magister: "Let salt consume what remains here."

With the broom, carefully brush excess salt across the whole ring.

> "I summon the hounds of the Dark Lord of the Mound to harrow whatever it finds here, to consume or return it to earth. So be it done."

He must then tip the cauldron of water over the salt ring, diffusing it into the earth. This ends the rite. All that needs to be done after this is to douse all the candles and fires. Gather everything up and just walk away. A small celebration afterwards is an uplifting climax and should be held as far away as possible from the place this was executed. There should be an instantly noticeable lift to the working site, the group and the individuals within it.

13
The
Poisoned
Chalice

Very occasionally, one encounters some rare object that is decorated with disparate images, seemingly at odds in concept with the overall design. One of these by 'chance' came into the possession of Robert Cochrane. Possibly composed of older symbolisms, its ornate design upon the chalice was primarily that of a skull entwined with roses. This pattern specifically and quite purposefully, combines the secrecy of the rose with the mystery of death, but in a totally different context than the combination of the rose and the grave. To begin with the chalice has always represented the feminine side of the Old Faith, the "*gynergy*" to be found in women, symbolized by the cup of wine carried by the Maid within the ritual circle.

When the Magister lowers the point of the knife into the chalice for the 'Houzle,' they are unabashedly mimicking a sexual union. Thus transformed, the wine embodies the very essence of life itself. The Maid then offers every member of the gathering a sip of the wine, symbolically a draft from the original Cauldron of Creation found within the Castle, where individual souls are sourced before being fixed within its new body at rebirth.

Now if the Maid that carries not the chalice, but the Horn as the Cornucopia, [thus representing the conjoined harmony of the crowned hermaphrodite] giving life to the body, we must not forget that She who generates life also holds death as Her greatest gift, for all life must mercifully end. All substance that sustains our lives comes from death, whether of animals or plants, and the skull on the cup reminds us of this. In death the last great secret of life is revealed and the promise enshrined in the symbol of the rose is revealed; and as we believe, the circle from birth to awaiting rebirth is travelled once again.

But witches love multiple meanings and the rose-skull chalice is often referred to enigmatically as the 'Poisoned Chalice.' It is not by accident that the way of the green sorcerer or shaman is often called: *"the poison path."*[58] Sometimes the matter of dosage is simply one of degree. Links between the Craft and shamanic traditions are ancient: the witch has knowledge of plants, and of course shamen have developed particular relationships with certain plants in order to access non-ordinary levels of reality. Within European witchcraft traditions particularly, the known plant allies Amanita muscaria, mandrake and others can be utterly fatal. For that reason, information on their use does not belong in the public remit. This would be irresponsible.

As an aside, we might add that the toxic nature of some of the flying ointments described by the lawyers and physicians involved in the witch trials of the fifteenth through the seventeenth centuries can be seen as a good argument for the existence of an 'Old Religion.' Very little information regarding the dosage or their attendant rites were ever written down. Hallucinatory plant ingredients can kill a person if not used with due caution; therefore, we suggest it is quite possible that someone must have been passing along the right information orally, 'mouth to ear.'

The 'Poisoned Chalice' then, is a sacred rite centred around a highly potent and symbolic image. In the past, when a person reached a certain point in his or her spiritual journey, they would have submitted themselves to this test. It must be stressed this was and is not something to be undertaken lightly nor is it something anyone should even attempt to persuade another person into doing as an experiment. The rite is also known as the Perilous Seat, because by tradition, persons undergoing this test must select a high and lonely place to take their 'perilous seat' just as the first evening stars appear during the dark of the Moon. They are presented with a chalice alleged to contain a mixture of wine and poison to be swallowed in one gulp.

Left alone all night, it is not until dawn breaks that their comrades who having spent the night in shelter, set off to retrieve them from their ordeal by spiritual fire. An old adage about the Perilous Seat says that a person undertaking it achieves one of three things: death, madness, or inspiration; and that accurately define it. Behind the rite of the 'Poisoned Chalice' is an ancient magical intention: to challenge the Fates in pursuit of knowledge. In laying open your life to Fate's decree, you have announced an acceptance and understanding of their role in the possible forfeiture of a life beholden to the Lady Herself, who in marking that moment in time to gather and take home your soul, has accepted your challenge to:

"Either take me-or **inspire** me."

Deprivation eats into your very soul even as its bodily sheath copes with the perishing effects of exposure; but this ancient tradition of mortifying the flesh is merely a short cut to spiritual development. There are many known parallels exampled within such rites of passage as found in the Sun Dance of the Plains Indians, or the Eastern practice of meditating under waterfalls or on surf-washed rocks. Extreme endurances exist in pious acts of self-mortification and of hair shirts and self-flagellation. All take as their initiating concept, the idea that physical suffering in a ritual setting can produce knowledge, wisdom and eventual salvation-or as we believe, the chance to see beyond this world, into the next. Indeed there are many precedents within myth and history of this. Pertinent to us, is the self-immolation of Woden upon the tree, wounded by lance and suffering the loss of one eye, the better to 'see' in the other reality, of a trance state.

In essence, the concept of challenging death as part of the mysteries fits in very well with the Clan Law:

"Do not do what you desire,
Do what is necessary.
Take all you are given,
Give all of yourself.
What I have, I Hold.
When all is lost,
And not until then,
Prepare to die with dignity."

In both cases, death is challenged with the intention of overcoming the final threshold as a barrier. It is to realise that death is but the next stage upon one's journey should She wish to claim you for it. This is the ultimate goal wherein the soul becomes part of the Godhead itself, and we become as gods.

POISONED CHALICE [AFTER JOHN]

Epilogue

In one of his letters to William Gray, Robert Cochrane wrote:

> "I am seriously considering leaving my group and working alone. I may sound dreadfully un-humble, but Jane and I have reached a stage where we can go faster by ourselves. The group is beginning to pull us backwards, and I for one would like to establish a new leader and move on myself. We have had a brilliant 'flash of light' recently that may lead to the end of an old era and the beginning of a new for us."

As this letter reveals, turning away from group workings to further develop one's own magical persona is not uncommon. Cochrane was at that stage about 1965, but things went horribly wrong, leading to his premature death. That particular tragedy however, in no way invalidates the concept that eventually one or two people will leave any group to continue its mysteries by working more intensely on their own. Some of these people may in fact become the shadow elders that Cochrane described in another letter:

> "We may be the last of the old school, but we still uphold the old attitudes and expect the same thing. Above we two rises another authority whose writ is far older than ours; to that authority we give absolute allegiance, and whose function is to train and work with us."

But he may also be referring to something far more enigmatic. The policy of Elders within any tradition holds true today just as it did in Cochrane's day and will continue to do so as long as the Clan of Tubal Cain exists. Only the Maid and the Magister will know and speak to them

145

because it is they who maintain the contact. When the Magister and Maid wish to withdraw from the Cuveen because they have reached a stage where working with the Cuveen is holding them back, subject to their elders' approval, they nominate their successors.

An elders' sole function is to watch, observe, and guide the direction of all groups and individuals within the Clan. If need be, when a gathering has been taken out of line, or in extreme cases, even where this may concern the Magister and Maid, the Elders must call for and place the transgressor/s 'under the sword.'[59] In effect, this means that such persons would be cast out of the *Clan fellowship* because the Elders serve as the guardians of the tradition even though in a sense they are not of it.

Although the idea of people leaving the coven to go off on their own may appear selfish, their spiritual experiences and magical development will filter back down into the working groups within the Clan through constant contact with their successors. Of course, this progression slowly changes the aims, attitudes, and directional evolution of the Clan, so we could say that the Tradition of Tubal Cain is always in a slow flux. In that regard it differs from many contemporary witchcraft groups who appear to stand still. This progressive yet steady rate of change is deliberate, being led by ancestral forces, so that in time, the Clan of Tubal Cain may not remain a 'witchcraft' group as we know it but something quite different.

Today the People of Goda of the Clan of Tubal Cain stands on the verge of another change in direction, just as Robert Cochrane predicted. This is not something that has come about in an arbitrary way but which has evolved gradually over six to eight years. Through our working of the four keys, we felt pushed by the Old Ones in a specific direction. What we did in Cochrane's time suited the psychic climate of that time; what we are doing now suits our time, and eventually, what we now do will

146

have out lived its usefulness. What will not change are the core concepts of the Stone Stile, the Cave of the Cauldron, the Castle of the Four Winds and the Chapel of the Grave, because they are the root stock on which the Clan of Tubal Cain through the **Star Crossed Serpent** was founded and handed on to Cochrane, who in turn passed to others. As long as the Clan survives, so will his name, for he was the one who introduced it to a wider public, the *first of his tradition* to do so.

Evan John Jones

Appendices:

Appendix 1

Robert Cochrane's Letters
To Robert Graves

Robert Cochrane was, by his own admission, an: *"admirer and a critic"* of the works of Robert Graves – particularly of: *The White Goddess* launched in 1948 it created quite a stir within academia that has scarce settled since. A work of exceptional poetic vision, it is loosely based upon historic fact, yet elucidates undeniable truths within the Mythopoetic worlds of the mystic, the poet and the mage.

More challenging yet than this was Grave's assertion that all inspiration flowed by grace of a capricious Muse, an ambivalent ice-queen, worshipped the world over in her many guises and various cults. Yet despite the book's frosty reception by his peers, it was lauded publically by his readers. Somehow, Graves tapped into a deep-rooted primal need to connect to the intangible and archetypal feminine noumena. Liberation was swift; an overwhelming surge of interest revived this Goddess Muse, elevating her in an unprecedented swing away from patriarchy, affecting the whole strata of magical belief, from folklore to the supernatural, now so firmly entrenched, it is almost inconceivable to imagine a different 'world view.' But, it was exactly this perspective that Robert Cochrane did in fact challenge Graves upon, boldly and quite self-assured.

Ironically, Robert Graves was also in correspondence with Gerald Gardner, who was expounding a very different kind of 'Craft' to that of Robert Cochrane during the 1960s. And although there is a plethora of material assumed to have been penned by Gerald Gardner, we have very few surviving letters or articles of Robert Cochrane's from which we may draw resourcefully or reliably upon. So the discovery of two additional letters expands our understanding of the *man* considerably (but not his work). Graves' book influenced both men considerably, but in entirely different ways. While Gardner used the material as an historical basis for his nature based religion: 'Wicca,' Cochrane exploited the resources both allegorically and analogically, allowing him to develop his teaching praxes substantially. Most especially he became very adept at setting riddles based on material from the book to test students upon their intuitive faculties and lateral cogniscence.

Cochrane discusses several unusual topics in fact, steering Graves into deeper revelation concerning his intuitive projections, with especial regard for the 'Black Goddess' with whom he is eager to opine some familiarity.[1] Some of Graves' views he berates and others he commends; but it is clear that whenever these were written, Cochrane intended a long and productive correspondence with Graves. Those familiar with Cochrane's other letters and articles will discern immediately particular themes of importance to his work, which is discussed in greater depth after the letters. The reader is first invited to peruse them carefully, making comparisons with his other works for indications of subjects known, understood and discussed. Collectively, this becomes extremely significant when we analyse to what purpose such scrutiny is served. Above everything, his anarchic passion, frustration, erudition and conviction spill out from the page, infusing the reader with the intense vigour of this most startling figure of 20th century.

Shani Oates

Letter One:

Dear Robert Graves,

I have read and re-read your book, 'The White Goddess,' with admiration, utter amazement and a taint of horror. I can see your point when you write of inspirational work, and realise that it must have resulted from quite an internal 'pressure,' since from my own experience, that is the way she works. However, I am just pointing out some other factors that might interest you in the manifestation of the 'Guiden Corn'. There is some evidence to support the theory that the British and French pagans believed in stages of spiritual development and maturity and had incorporated this into their religious beliefs. There is still in existence a carved dolmen in Brittany that has all the witch symbols and mysteries arrayed upon it, surmounted by a carving in the round of Christ, which archeologists describe as a depiction of the passion of Christ. It dates from 1674 and to the best of my knowledge, (I come from an old witch family and although the family's beliefs were moribund at my fathers birth, I know enough to get along) the carving is anything but Christian. In this carving there is the eight circles with death supporting the bell Goddess above them. These, so I was told, represent the eight states or worlds of manifestation, and since they appear to correspond with Jungian psychology which is a rehash of much of the mystery systems, the rest is quite interesting. Also there are other factors connected with this ninefold unfolding of the spirit. There is amongst many, an old m.s in which an epic hero by the name of Libius Disconis undertakes nine adventures accompanied by Ellen and one dwarf. In these adventures all the enemies defeated are of the true mythological flavour, and Libius evidently ends by releasing the Goddess in one of her most dangerous forms and marrying her. However it is the progress of Tannhauser in its original form. The damned thing eludes me, since I am unable to make up my mind whether it is seasonal or psychological. I would be interested to hear of what you can make of it. It has the advantage of the various tribal animals and heroes of the Druidical system in corporated in it, and it may possibly be an opening to the mystery that still surrounds much of the iconography of the Old Religion.

Incidentally, the battle of the trees may also be a system equivalent to the tree system of twelfth century magic. There are many points in common between the Hermatic and Kabbalists meditational system and the trees of Talisien. A friend of mine has claimed that he has worked it out, but until it fits to the endocrine glands of the body, I personally cannot see how this can be so. The Kabbalistic Tree of Life along with the book of Thoth seems to belong more to Appollo than the Goddess. I think that you are absolutely right when you say that she is the prime source of inspiration.

Yours sincerely,

R.L. Bowers.

P.S. My apologies for writing, but I have found so much of interest in your books that I almost feel that you are an old friend.

Letter Two:

Dear Robert Graves,

Thank you for your unexpected and very welcome letter. I find your point about the influx of the Islamic societies interesting, but apart from Gerald Gardner's covens and Idris Shah, I have not heard of it before. I have been told that my grandfather's grandfather dressed in skins and horned head-dress for ritual practice since he was an 'Old Man', (high priest, devil, what you will,) I fail to see that Islamic practice or belief had reached so far, since, as you will know, the Sufi and kindred societies did not enact the part of God; Their aim was to achieve a mystical state *vide* various practices. To the best of my knowledge, that was not the aim of the Staffordshire and Warwickshire witches. Flags, flax, fodder and Frig was their total aim, good crops, healthy children and some power to strike back at the oppressor was the aim, and in my opinion they succeeded. There was poetry, there was mysticism, but these were either side effects or something that belonged to the individual rather than the group. However, there may be a very distinct difference between the witches of the west and of the midlands. They still used the triple stave or 'stang', and used deer antlers, not bull horns for certain purposes (Incidentally the stag of seven tines may have a meaning to each of the tines), and to the best of my knowledge they did not use the ritual star, or the binding thereof as part of their ritual, instead they used the deathshead and bones. I agree that there has been an influx of Eastern magic and mysticism, but the question is upon the distance that it spread. In my personal opinion there are two distinct kinds of witches (and taking into account the events over the last fifteen years, three kinds) and it may be that they lived in mutual toleration of each other. However, according to some research I have done upon this particular branch, it mayhap that this division was originally social, and there is quite a difference between the peasant and the squires mysteries. I leave it to your superior knowledge to see whether there is any truth in this statement. But as a sort of interesting side line, there is pretty good evidence that the gypsies infiltrated into the English clans, and for that matter else where. They may have carried various Indian practices with them. The whole ruddy subject gets so confusing that I usually end up with fresh knowledge about something that I had no intention of examining. Still it is something that once picked up, you can't put it down again. I sometimes feel when I am wandering around in the marshes of the old knowledge, that the dam upstream is going to burst and the whole of humanity is going to be submerged by fifty thousand years of pre-history, swamping the neat subtopian conventions of the last thousand years. King Log has already sunk, but they still worship the memory.

I was interested in your description (one of the difficulties of communication – 'interested'!) of the physical appearance of the Goddess symptons (Gawd, my spelling). I am not biased towards the poetical aspect but more towards the Black Goddess, so my knees do not shake or eyes run, but I do get a sudden feeling of intense pressure, something like an approaching storm. It is as you say a physical thing, almost a desire to run and find shelter. I have also 'seen' the Goddess, although She was riding a white horse, maybe it was artistic vision, I do not know, but I was genuinely terrified for the following week. At the present moment I have the best of both worlds with the Black and the White. . . Of course I will pay for it later, hire purchase is no new thing . . .

Yours sincerely, R.L. Bowers.

References:

i.   Robert Graves died in 1985 while in Mallorca, his many correspondences were systematically filed and logged for future historic use. Discovered among biographical research material, by the esteemed writer Grevel Lindop, to whom I owe a debt of gratitude for his kindness and co-operation in publishing these two undated letters. Professor Lindop states that although "both are poorly typed, and unedited for clarity (now held by the St John's College Robert Graves Trust)" we now have another facet of this enigmatic persona to explore.

They are assumed by Lindop to have not been written prior to 1963, possibly because Cochrane's subject references in the letters to the 'Black Goddess' had not yet been made public until Graves discussed her within his lectures of that year. Graves' views on the Black Goddess also formed the basis of the book published in 1965: *Mammon and the Black Goddess.* Cochrane raises this figure with Graves, coaxing further discussion upon the paradox of her contrasting nature with the White Goddess.

Appendix 2

Smith-Craft And The Cunning-Art

ANVIL: Old English: *anfealt*

The modern English word anvil developed from this early form: *anfealt* which has its origin in the Proto-Indo-European root *pel. If we study the origin of the word anvil as an attempt to learn why the smith and smith craft has been so esteemed and venerated as possessing something 'other,' there is an abundance of astonishing information and confirmation as to the magical and possible priestly/ kingly role of a person who is able to fashion by force of wit and will a weapon to defend as easily as a plough to plunder and fecund the earth. For many decades much speculation has surrounded the word commonly associated with the role of cunning-person in the title of 'peller/pellar.'

But if we look very closely at the following list of associations and derivatives (included for interested parties to explore to their own satisfaction), then a better and more logical attribution would be the more obvious 'smith' whose trade and tools coincidently derive from the same stem root as pellar, encompassing, the force and skill required to temper both *steel and tongue* – master of the word (spirit of fire) and the forge (manifest fire). It is perhaps easy to see the historical and folk link of a blacksmith with a magus, a horseman and a toad-man. Least likely is the term *ex*peller given the requisite prefix to make sense of the term and the shift away from the link between the smith, his tools and his horse - both iron (relating to anvil) and breath (spirit). Thus, wielding the three civilizing arts of field, structure and warfare, it is not but a shuffle to imagine the valorisation of such a mage and even veneration as priest/ king?

I should however stress that the service and function of an *'expeller'* is not to be discounted from the usage associated with the development and practises of the peller ...and it would be another valuable expression and development finding usage of the stem 'pel', but the primary dynamic offering the greatest significance, particularly to Cainite Traditions is clearly the synthesis and elegance of the smith and his craft (including the command of the spoken word, especially through the horseman's and toads-man's word) and is too fine a fit to pass over.

1. Proto-Indo-European root *pel-

    English anvil, Greek pelargos, Latin pallere,

2. Proto-Indo-European root *pel- derived from the Proto-Indo-European root *pel-

    English fold, French faldestoel, High German faldan, Italian falda, Latin -plus

    Proto-Indo-European root *pel- derived from the Proto-Indo-European root *pel-

    Derivations in other languages

    English felting, Greek plesios, Latin appellare, Latin compellare, Latin filtrum, Latin polire, Latin pellere

3. the Latin word *pellere* (beat; drive out; push) derived from the Proto-Indo-European root *pel-

4. the Latin word appellare (call; address; dun) derived from the Proto-Indo-European root *pel-

5. the Latin word pallere (be, look pale; fade) derived from the Proto-Indo-European root *pel-[60]

    Looking at its development in speech now:

Part of Speech: noun. Pronunciation: [pê-'lem-ik]

Definition:

(1)The art of debate and argumentation.

(2) a passionate defense or refutation of an argument.

Usage: This word can entail a negative connotation but need not actually be negative, however. A polemic could be simply a passionate argument.

Etymology:

The modern term 'polemic' started out as Greek *polemikos* "hostile," the adjective from polemos "war, battle." The root of the Greek word originally meant "beat, hit, thrust." The same root turns up in Old English "*anfealt,*" which today is "anvil," something you beat on. Old English "felt" is also a relative that may have been borrowed into medieval Latin as the root in filtrum "felt, filter," which returned to English as "filter." In Latin the original root became pellere "to push, drive, hit," whose past participle is pulsus "beat" from which we derive "pulse." [61]

7. expel, v. t. [L. expellere, expulsum; ex out + pellere to drive: cf.F. expeller.

    [See also: Pulse- a beat.].

a. To drive or force out from that within which anything is contained, enclosed, or situated; to eject; as, to expel air from a bellows. [1913 Webster]

b. To drive away from one's country; to banish. [1913 Webster]

c. To cut off from further connection with an institution of learning, a society, and the like; as, to expel a student or member. [1913 Webster]

d.   To keep out, off, or away; to exclude. Shak. [1913 Webster]

e.   To discharge; to shoot. [1913 Webster]

f.   Syn. — To banish; exile; eject; drive out. [62]

Nicholaj de Mattos Frisvold confirms this use:

"The idea of pellar craft being crafted on exorcisms/ purifications is in harmony with the perspective held in medieval Christianity in Iceland and Norway as well, where it is mentioned in for instance The Galdrabok the existence of Svartskinnr and Raudskinnr, said to be powerful books of sorcery - often manipulated by bishops and priests. These powerful books were of course, Svartskinnr - Black skin = The Holy Bible and Raudskinnr - Red skin -The Book of Exorcisms. Of course a part of the 'black books' were not the Bible per se, but Kunstbøker (Art books) and Syphrianer/Cyprian's, but the Red Book was most likely related to the secrets of the pellar - or 'ex-pellar'."

Ex-pellers are therefore frequently presented as Cunning folk, but maybe not always. Cunning derives from the Anglo-Saxon root 'cunnan' - to know. Wizard, similarly derives from the Old English 'wis' - meaning wise, hence wise-man. These were individuals who were seen as being in some way 'different' from those around them. They had knowledge and gifts, that in times past were perceived as hereditary, or even obtained from a supernatural source, generally from the Fey, the Faerie folk. In their world, folk custom and tradition provided the context for their everyday lives, for their beliefs and superstitions, and for which we have no parallel in this century. It is impossible to estimate the saturation level or the import and influence these values instigated. This is completely alien to the modern mind. Early Viking and Anglo-Saxon accounts describe these 'cunning-folk' or wise-men under the blanket term 'Wiccan,' believed to have been pronounced *'Wichen,'* that has since devolved into the more derogatory term 'wytch.' Encompassed within the term *'Wiccan,'* are the variant practises of hexcraft and *'drycroeft'* that covered all manner of sorceries, divination, healing and spell craft.

Certainly both terms have merit, both have recourse to magic, but only one of them enjoins the practises of smith-craft with the magical arts and of Cainite theology.

Appendix 3

Lay of the Nine Herbs [1]

The famous *'Lay of the Nine Herbs'* shows how Woden smote the 'serpent' and how its nine fragments produced nine diseases, which may be neutralized by the nine herbs found within the charm. Native Teutonic peoples possessed an innate sense of *'mana,'* apparent within the words: *'miht,' 'maegen'* and *'craeft,'* all of which awarded beneficent power. *'Elfshot'* is the flying venom, disease and corruption subject to the malefic 'power' of sorcerers. In order that this charm may be fully appreciated, it is reproduced here. [63]

'Have thou in mind, Mugwort, what thou didst reveal,

What thou didst establish at the mighty denunciation.[i]

Una[ii] is thy name, oldest of herbs.

Thou art strong against three, and against thirty.

Thou art strong against venom, and against onflight.[iii]

Thou art strong against the evil She, [iv]
that fareth throughout the land.

And thou Waybroad,[v] Mother of herbs,

From eastwood open, mighty within.

Over thee, chariots have rumbled,
over thee Queens have ridden,

Over thee brides cried out, over thee bulls have snorted.

All didst thou then withstand, and dost confound:

So do thou withstand venom and the onflight

And that evil thing that fareth throughout the land.

Stune[vi] is this herb named, on stone hath she grown.

She standeth against venom, pain she assaulteth

Stithe is her name, venom she confoundeth,

She driveth forth the evil things, casteth out venom.

This is the herb which hath fought against snake.[vii]

This is strong against venom, she is strong against the onflight,

She is strong against those evil things that fare throughout the land.

Rout thou now Attorlothe,[viii] the less route the greater,

The greater the less, until to him be remedy from both.[ix]

Have thou in mind, Maythe, what thou didst reveal,

What thou didst bring to pass at Allerford,

That never for flying ill did ye yield up his life.

Since for him Maythe was made ready for his eating.

This is the plant that Wergule[x] is named,

This did the seal send forth over the high sea,

As cure[xi] for the wrath of another venom.[xii]

There did apple and venom bring it about

That she never would turn into the house.[xiii]

Chervil and fennel, great and mighty two,

These herbs did the wise Lord[xiv] create,

Holy in the heavens when he hung;

He stablished[xv] and sent them into the seven worlds,

For poor and rich, for all a remedy.[xvi]

This standeth against pain, this assaulteth[xvii] venom,

This is strong against three and against thirty,

Against bewitchment [xviii]by little things.

Now these nine herbs avail against nine spirits of evil,

Against nine venoms and against nine onfliers,

Against the red venom, against the foul venom,

Against the white venom, against the purple venom,

Against the yellow venom, against the green venom,

Against the livid venom, against the blue venom,

Against the brown venom, against the crimson venom;

(Pagan lay of the Magic Blasts)

Against 'worm' blister, against water blister,

Against thorn blister, against thistle blister,

Against ice blister, against venom blister,

If any venom flying from the east, or from the north[xix] assailing come,

Or from the west over the race of man.

Christ[xx] stood above the ancient ones, the malignant ones.

I alone know the running streams,

And the nine adders now they guard.

All weeds must now give way to herbs;

Seas must disperse, all salt water must disperse,

When I this venom from thee blow.'

(How to use the Lays)

Mugwort, waybroad facing the morning Sun, lambscress, attorlothe, maythe, nettle, wild crabapple, chervil, fennel and old soap. Work the plants to dust, mingle with soap and the juice of the apple. Make a slime of water and ashes. Take fennel, boil in the slime and foment with the mixture when the salve is applied, both before and after. Sing the charm upon each of the plants thrice before working up, and upon the apple in like manner. And let one sing into the man's mouth and both ears and into the wound that same charm before the salve be applied.

The Nine Herbs Charm is one of the spells contained in the

'Lacnunga' ('the Cures'), a collection of Anglo-Saxon healing charms written down around 1000 C.E. It's an "herb-song", a poem that was recited as herbs were collected and/or prepared for use. Such charms were routinely forbidden in medieval 'Penitentials'. For example, the Corrector of Burchard of Worms (1008 CE) includes the question:

> "Hast thou collected medicinal herbs with evil incantations, not with the Creed and the Lord's prayer, that is, with the singing of the "credo in Deum" and the Paternoster ["Our Father"]? If thou hast done it otherwise [than with the Christian formulae mentioned] thou shalt do penance for ten days on bread and water."

There are a lot of textual problems with the charm as both versions here reveal. Words, phrases or whole lines are different or simply missing. And they include less than nine herbs; they leave out one of the four directions, etc. Most of the stories it refers to have been forgotten. Academics are still unsure exactly what herbs are referred to. But together, they express a resonance, a feel for the 'charming' practises of its period.

Despite the more obvious later Christian interpolations, this charm retains much of its original virtues and clearly demonstrates the Anglo-Saxon obsession with nines, flying venom and the worm, all neatly extricated within the verse. It is important to note, that many healing activities in 'shamanic' societies such as these, involved 'combat' with the disease, often adjured in the name of a powerful local deity (specific to their clan) to depart; these later became adopted for the rites of exorcism.[64] Another academic remarks that in Cockayne's 'Leechbook', special power is attributed to all herbs that grow in graveyards and burial grounds.[65]

Classical sources also advise on plant magic, their gathering and administration, which subject to Oriental (Persian, Chaldean, Babylonian and Assyrian via Hellenistic Greece) influences also adopted greater astrological associations. Synthesized within the extant Anglo-Saxon magical superstitions, these potent incantations were eventually banned in the 6th and early 13th centuries.

Instructions developed curious rituals in order to safeguard both plant and its gatherer. Some simply involved averting one's gaze, as with sea holly, others required circles to be drawn around the plant, some required use of iron, others eschewed it, almost all were subject to Moon or planetary alignments and phases. Reverence of and taboos surrounding iron are replete within the *'Lacnunga'* with special observance to treatment of wounds dealt with by iron. Iron's magnetic and mystical associations assured a special reverence too for the smiths that worked it, as the following lines within this narrative charm against *'elfshot'* clearly reveal.[66]

The Nine Herbs Charm [2]

Lay of the Nine Herbs

Be mindful, Mugwort, what you did reveal,

What you did arrange at Regenmeld.[i]

Una[ii] you are called, oldest of herbs,

You are strong against three and against thirty,

You are strong against poison and against onfliers[iii] [flying venoms]

You are strong against the loathsome foe[iv] who fares through the land.

And you, Waybroad[v] [Plantain], Mother of herbs,

Open from the east, mighty within.

Over you chariots creaked, over you queens rode,

Over you brides cried out, over you bulls snorted.

All this you did withstood, and resist.

So you withstand poison and flying venom,

And the loathsome foe who fares through the land.

Stune[vi] this herb is called, she grew on a stone,

She stands against poison, she attacks pain.

Stithe [hard] she is called, she confounds poison,

She drives out evils, she casts out poison.

This is the herb that fought against the worm[vii],

This is strong against poison, she is strong against flying venoms,

She is strong against the loathsome foe who fares through the land.

Rout you now, Attorlathe[viii] [Venomloather], though you are the lesser,

You the mightier, conquer the lesser the more, until he be rid of both.[ix]

Remember you, Maythe [Camomile], what you revealed,

What you accomplished at Alorford,

That never for flying venom did he yield life

166

Since for him a man prepared Maythe for food.

 This is the herb that is called Wergule.[x]

This a seal sent over the sea ridges,

To heal the harm of other venoms.

[Two herbs, chervil and fennel, are missing]

[Lay of the Nine Twigs of Woden]

These nine go against nine poisons.

A worm came crawling, he wounded nothing.[xi]

Then Woden took nine glory-twigs[xii] [wuldor tanas]

Smote then the adder that it flew apart into nine (parts).

There apple and poison brought it about

That she never would dwell in the house. [xiii]

Chervil and Fennel, very mighty two,

These herbs the wise Lord [Drighten][xiv]

Holy in the heavens wrought while He hung;

He established and sent them into the seven worlds,

To the poor and the rich, for all a remedy.

She stands against pain, she assaults poison,

Who has power against three and against thirty,

Against a fiend's[xv] hand and against sudden trick,

Against the witchcraft[xvi] of vile wights.[xvii]

Now these nine herbs have power against nine evil spirits[xviii]

[wuldorgeflogenum, "fugitives from glory"],

Against nine poisons and against nine flying venoms:

Against the red poison, against the foul poison,

Against the white poison, against the purple poison,

Against the yellow poison, against the green poison,

Against the dark poison, against the blue poison,

Against the brown poison, against the crimson poison.

 Against worm-blister, against water-blister,

Against thorn-blister, against thistle-blister,

Against ice-blister, against poison-blister.

If any poison flying from the east,[xix]

Or any from the north . . . come

Or any from the west over all mankind.

Christ[xx] stood over the old ones, the malignant ones[?]

I alone know running streams

Where the nine adders keep guard[?]

All weeds must now give way to herbs

the seas slip apart, all salt water,

when I this poison blow from you.

[The Preparation]

Mugwort, waybroad open from the east, lamb's cress, attorlathe, maythe, nettle, crab-apple, chervil and fennel, old soap; work the herbs into dust, mix them with the soap and the apple juice. Work then a paste of water and of ashes; take fennel, boil it in the paste and beat with the [herbal] mixture when he applies the salve both before and after. Sing the charm [galdor] on each of the herbs three times before he prepares them, and on the apple likewise. And let someone sing into the mouth of the man and into both his ears, and on the wound, that same charm [galdor] before he applies the salve.

[Translated by Karen Louise Jolly. Uni. Carolina]

Notes

i.   Regenmeld means "Great Council" and may not be a proper noun. A Christian interpretation makes it Jesus' last pronouncements before the ascension (Mark 16:18). Some translators just leave it as "Regenmeld", since it might be a place, too.

ii.   Una – unknown herb, possibly another name for Mugwort.

iii.   "Onfliers" is *onflyge* (literally, "thing flying upon"). Could be the "elf-dart" referred to in Germanic as Mugwort. Generic – not specific.

iv.   The "loathesome foe" is probably a personification of infectious disease, which was often described as a spirit or demon flying through the night.

v. *Wegbrade*, "way-bread", is plantain or dock.

vi. This herb is called Stune; it grew on a stone, it withstands poison, it resists pain. It is called 'harsh', it fights against poison, drives out the hostile one, casts out poison. Stune may be lamb's cress.

vii. The Worm, is the mighty serpent, the destructive forces of nature personified in the mythical dragon.

viii. These last two sentences very corrupt in the poem. Though the sense is clear: *attorlathe* ("poison-hater") is the weaker poison than the poison afflicting the victim, yet it will destroy the 'greater' poison and is thus the greatest.

ix. Uncertain as to what herb *attorlathe* is. Most suggest cock's-spur grass but betony is another possibility.

x. Once again, the herb is obscure. Crab-apple and nettle are both possibilities.

xi. Literally, "*toslat he nan*" – it slayed no one. But most people correct this to "it bit a man".

xii. Glory-twigs are probably small staves with Runes carved on them.

xiii. Meaning obscure...

xiv. The hanging lord might be Christ, Woden, or both seen as the same.

xv. Fiend is literal – *feond*, a Christian demon; though the word can also simply mean an enemy.

xvi. Witchcraft is *malscrunge*. It could also be translated as 'enchantment' or 'charm.'

xvii. Evil beings is *manra wihta*, "of evil wights" - any sort of being, natural or supernatural.

xviii. Evil spirits is *wuldorgeflogenum*, literally "those who have fled from glory".

xix. Another corrupt section. South is absent.

xx. Many people see Christ as a late addition. It fits poorly with the poem's meter.

Appendix 4

Rosary/Prayer Beads

Scented chaplets and rosaries have been devotional aids to contemplation of the divine for several millennia within many cultures, having arcane virtue and tactile stimulus. Often of knotted thread, seeds, wood or bone, they combine aesthetics with organic harmonics. Royalty often composed their ropes of precious or semi-precious stones, terminated by a specific symbol wrought in gold or silver. Each set of beads is numbered significantly according to deific assignation, denoting the number of sacred names, or mysteries associated with them. The total number of beads is then divided into repetitive sets, marked by spacer beads, such that the hand registers them subconsciously during use - a subliminal reminder to repeat the invocations and/or advance another level of chant or mantra. As an efficient meditational tool they facilitate trance and focus in the dedication of your chosen purpose and are also perfectly suited to serve as worry beads.

How to make your own chaplet

Decide first of all the potency to whom you wish to dedicate your beads, as this will determine its design. A little research will assist you in this.

Roses, for example sacred to Aphrodite, provide a beautiful and meaningful core upon which to construct your beads. Her number is six, with 3x6 forming a link to Venus aspected as Fate. Therefore 18 beads + 3 spacers, will be required, totalling 21 (acquiring a value that reduces to 3 using numerology, bringing the virtue back to the triune form of Fate pertinent to this dedication).

These may be achieved as follows:

1. Gather fresh petals during a waxing Moon (on a Friday, under the light of Venus, visible during this autumn in the early hours of the morning), at least several cups full. Cover with only enough water to prevent exposure to air. Steep for an hour over a low heat in a sturdy pan, each day for three consecutive days. Once cool, mould the blackened pulp into small beads with well oiled fingers scented with 3 drops of rose otto (absolute, if you can afford it) dispersed in 10ml of almond oil. Thread carefully via a sharp needle, preferably onto organic yarn, strong wool, or cotton. As they shrivel and dry, turn them each day to keep them mobile on the yarn. Make larger beads as spacers if desired and tie off with a tassel or small charm (ankh, pentacle, etc)

2. Alternatively, again gather petals as above. Place in a pestle and add previously ground spikenard (believed to be of the aromatic ginsing, valerian or lavender families), myrrh, (both in ratio of 1:4 of petals) dried costus (another aromatic rhizome related to the ginger family popular within ayurvedic medicine) and orris root (traditional fixative, ground from the iris bulb)(both in ratio of 1:8 of rose petals). Pound together, then add enough runny honey to bind them together. Form beads and thread as before. Leave to dry somewhere ambient until hard.

3. Crushed dried spices (sweet or hot) may be combined with gums and oils such as benzoin, storax, almond or even glycerine to which essential oils (of choice) such as frankincense, sandalwood, vetivert, rose, neroli, vanilla etc may be added, again 3-5 drops per 10ml of gum or oil. Form into beads and thread as above into desired order.

4. Finally, and my personal favourite, gather rose-hips and haws, again

173

under the aegis of Venus; thread haws while plump onto strong yarn into relevant pattern, using the larger rose-hips as spacers. Hang in a warm room but out of direct light and allow it to dry. If no spacers are required, the rose-hips alone make a spectacular chaplet. Once dried they may be oiled lightly each day over seven days with scented oil as in #1 until burnished and beautifully perfumed.

Appendix 5

Fava alla Romagna (Roman broad beans)

½ pound of flour, ¼ pound of sugar ¼ pound sweet almonds, 1 ounce of butter, 1 egg, 1 egg yolk, flavouring of lemon, orange, or cinnamon, as desired, a little brandy.

Blanch and skin the almonds and pound in a bowl with the sugar until they resemble grains of rice. Lightly beat the whole egg, then add it and the flour to the almonds. Thoroughly mix, adding enough brandy to make a stiff dough. Roll out and shape pieces into large broad "beans." Place them on a buttered tray and sprinkle with a little flour. Brush the "beans" with the lightly beaten egg yolk and place in a moderate oven (350-375 degrees F.) for five to ten minutes, until they are a pale golden colour.

You now have a traditional dish that was once used as an offering to the departed as part of the feast of the dead. Made at All Hallow's Eve, what better way to end a ritual by passing these around instead of the usual apple?

Bibliography:

'Arabi, Ibn. *'The Tree of Being: an Ode to the Perfect Man'* 2005 Archetype Cambridge

Ashe, G. *'Mythology of the British Isles'* 2002 Methuen Pub. Ltd. London

Awn, P. J. *'Satan's Tragedy and Redemption: Iblis in Sufi Psychology'* 1983 Leiden: E.J.Brill

Bayley, Harold. *'The Lost language of Symbolism'* 2006 Dover Publications NY

Bauval, R. & Gilbert, A. *'The Orion Mystery'* 1994 Arrow Books. UK

Bettelheim, B. *'The Uses of Enchantment: Meaning and Importance of Fairy Tales'* 1976. Thames & Hudson London.

Bonfante, Larissa. & Swaddling, Judith. *'Etruscan Myths'* 2006 British Museum Press UK p48

Burne, C.S. *'The Handbook of Folklore'* 1996 Senate London

Bushaway, B. *'By Rite: Custom, Ceremony and Community in England 1700-1880'* 1982 Junction Books London

Campbell, Joseph. *'The Mythic Image'* 1974 MJF Books. USA

Doel, G&F. *'Mumming, Howling and Hoodening'* 1992 Headly Bros. Kent.

Drury, Neville & Skinner, Stephen. *'The Search for Abraxas.'* 1972 Neville Spearman Ltd London

Flint, Valerie. *'The Rise of Magic in Early Medieval Europe'* 1991 New Jersey, Princeton Uni. Press

Goblet d' Alviella, Count Eugene. *'Symbols: Their Migration and Universality'* 2000 Dover UK

Gratten, J.H.G. & Singer, C. *'Anglo-Saxon Magic and Medicine.'*, 1952, Oxford Uni. Press.

Guénon, René. *'Symbols of Sacred Science'* 2004 Sophia Perennis NY

Guénon, René. *'King of the World'* 2004 Sophia Perennis NY

176

Harte, J. *'Explore Fairy Traditions'* 2004 Heart of Albion Press UK

Harvey, Andrew. *'Rumi: Love's Glory'* 1996 Balthazar Books San Francisco

Incantus, Theosaurus*: 'The Spagyric Quest of Beroaldus Cosmopolita'* Wyman & Sons. London

Hole, C. *'British Folk Customs'* 1976 Hutchinson & Co. London

Hutton, Professor Ronald. *'The Triumph of the Moon'* 1999 Oxford Uni Press.

Jackson, Nigel. *'Celestial Magic'* 2003 Capall Bann UK

Jones, E. J. & Clifton, C. *'Sacred Mask, Sacred Dance'* 1997 Llwellyn Pub. USA

Jones, E. J. *'The Roebuck in the Thicket'* (ed) Howard, M. 2001 Capall Bann. Berks

Jones, E.J. *'The Robert Cochrane Letters'* (ed) Howard. M. 2002 Capall Bann. Berks

Jurich, M. *'Scheherazade Sisters: Trickster Heroines'* 1998 Greenwood Press Westport

Kieckhefer, R. *'Magic in the Middle Ages'* 2000, Cambridge Uni. Press.

Larner, C. *'Witchcraft and Religion'* 1986 Oxford Uni Press.

Laroque, F. *'Shakespeare's Festive World'* 1993 Cambridge Uni. Press.

Levy, Gertrude. *'The Gate of Horn'* 1953 Faber & Faber London

Leland, Charles Godfrey. *'Popular Roman Etruscan Remains'* 1892 T. Fisher-Unwin. UK

Liddell, W.E. *'The Pickinghill Papers'* (ed) Howard. M. 1994 Capall Bann. Berks

Maple, E. *'Cunning Murrell: A Study of a 19th Century Cunning-man in Hadleigh'* 1960 Folklore #71 pp. 36-43

Marvelly, Paula. *'Women of Wisdom.'* 2005 Watkins UK

Muchembled, R. *'A History of the Devil from the Middle Ages to the Present'* 2003 Polity Press. UK

Oates, Shani. *Tubelo's Green Fire.'* 2010 Mandrake of Oxford UK

Palmer, R. *Britain's Living Folklore'* 1995 Llanerch Pub. Felinfach

Patai, Raphael. *The Hebrew Goddess'* 1990 Wayne State Uni press.

Porteous, A. *'Folklore of the Forest: Myths and Legends'* 1996 Senate. London

Purkiss, Diana. *A Witch in History'* 1996 Routledge UK

Radford, E&M.A. *Ency. of Superstitions'* (ed) Hole. C. 1974 BCA. GB

Readers Digest Ass. (ed) *Folklore, Myths and Legends of Britain'* 1973 London

Roberts, J. (ed) *Oxford Dictionary of the Classical World'* 2005 Oxford

Roud, S. *The English Year'* 2008 Penguin England

Russell, J. B. *The Devil'* 1987 Cornell Uni. Press. USA.

Simpson, J. & Westwood, J. *The Lore of the Land: a Guide to England's Legends'* 2005 Penguin. England

Simpson, J. *'Legends of the Chanctonbury Ring'* 1969 Folklore #80 pp122-131

Spence, Lewis. *'The Mysteries of Britain'* 1994 Senate Paperbacks. UK p218

Valiente, D. *Rebirth of Witchcraft'* 1989 Hale. London

Valiente, D. *ABC of Witchcraft'* 1984 Hale. London

Valiente, D. *Witchcraft for Tomorrow'* 1985 Hale. London

Wagner, Dr. W. *Asgard and the Gods'* 2010 Lightning Source Ltd.UK

Whitlock, R. *Guide to British Folklore: In search of Lost Gods'* 1979 Phaidon, UK

Williamson, John. *The Holly and Oak Kings'* 1987 Harper Collins UK

www.sacredtexts.com/cdshop/indexhtm chapter 13

www.feri.com/dawn/voluspa

http://en.wikipedia.org/wiki/Norse_mythology

http://fmg.ac/Projects/MedLands/

ENGLAND,%20AngloSaxon%20&%20Danish%20Kings.htm

www.digital.library.unt.edu/permalink/meta-dc-3694:1

www.scribd.com/doc/2396347/The-Flourishing-of-Romance-and-the-

Rise-of-AllegoryPeriods-of-European-Literature

www.historicroses.org

www.India.net

http://net.bible.org/lexicon.php?word=expel

http://www.myetymology.com/

http://www.templeofsolomon.org/Etablet.htg/emerald_tablet.htm

http://en.wikipedia.org/wiki/Germanic_peoples

http://www.mythfolklore.net/india/encyclopedia/varuna.htm

http://www.speakwithoutinterruption.com/site/2009/03/leadership/

www.plexoft.com/SBF/green.grow.html

www.hymnsandcarolsofchristmas.com/.../green_grow_the_rushes.html

www.hedgewytchery.com/songs_chants.html

Robert Cochrane Resources:

Internet:

http://www.cyberwitch.com/bowers This official website is authorized to display enhanced texts of all articles written by Robert Cochrane for The Pentagram and New Dimensions in the 1960s, as well as some of his correspondence.

http://www.clanoftubalcain.org.uk Official & Unequivocal Holders of Virtue, Title and Legacy of the Clan of Tubal Cain, instated, blessed and sanctioned by E.J. Jones.

www.1734-witchcraft.org Official Website of Doyens of Joseph Wilson Teachings.

Books about Robert Cochrane, 1734, and the Clan of Tubal Cain

Shani Oates, *'Tubelo's Green Fire.'* Mandrake of Oxford. 2010

Justine Glass, *'Witchcraft: The Sixth Sense.'* Robert Cochrane is the *'Magister'* referred to in several chapters.

Ronald Hutton, *The Triumph of the Moon: A History of Modern Pagan Witchcraft*' (Oxford University Press, 1999). In chpt. 16, entitled "The Man in Black." Prof. Ronald Hutton records his summary of modern British Traditional Craft.

William G. Gray, *Western Inner Workings.*' (York Beach, Maine: Samuel Weiser, 1983). William Gray and Robert Cochrane admired and influenced each other's work considerably.

William G. Gray, *Seasonal Occult Rituals*' (London: Aquarian Press, 1970).

Evan John Jones and Chas S. Clifton. *Sacred Mask, Sacred Dance*' (St. Paul: Llewellyn, 1997).

Doreen Valiente, *The Rebirth of Witchcraft*' (London: Robert Hale, 1989). The late Doreen Valiente devotes a complete chapter to Robert Cochrane, based on her own brief experiences within the Clan of Tubal Cain.

Doreen Valiente and Evan John Jones, *Witchcraft: A Tradition Renewed*' (Custer, Washington: Phoenix Publishing, 1990). These former members of Cochrane's Clan of Tubal Cain devised this working system based on and around their work with Robert Cochrane, taking it out to the public.

E. J. Jones and Michael Howard, *The Roebuck in the Thicket*' Capall Bann 2001, edited version of Jones' original manuscript covering Clan workings at a deeper level. Five published articles by Robert Cochrane supplement this work.

E. J. Jones and Michael Howard, *The Robert Cochrane Letters*' Capall Bann 2003, another work edited by Mike Howard. A consolidation of most of the correspondences of Robert Cochrane, with notes.

Notes to Volume I

1   E. J. Jones & Mike Howard [ed] 'The Roebuck in the Thicket' 2001 Capall Bann UK

2   See appendix 1

3   In fact, this gentle evaluation is here given to avoid the contentious issue at that time with how She was perceived by a mainly American readership the original ms was designated for.

4   Like Robert Cochrane before him, E. J. Jones used the word witch grudgingly.

5   Here it is the oak tree and not the season that is important [which is a lapwing]. See Chapter 'The Stang'

6   Extant within many Craft traditions, though not all. Even then, the sacrificial King concept here is not necessarily one borne by orthodox history. Divine twins formulate the mythos of the Young Horn King, one Tanist and discarnate whose manifest counterpart is the incarnating twin of light – Lucifer.

7   The raven is in fact Munnin, or memory, one of the two companions of Odhin, whose significance once we cross the Lethe, or river of forgetfulness, will not be missed.

8   As one able to traverse beyond both the corporeal and metaphysical bounds of the 'quick and the dead' respectively, in life and after death.

9   very revealingly Gnostic!

10   Who are most generally considered as being the long dead shades of our ancestors, for others, these are aspects of various deities

now long forgotten by the Christian world, and for some, they are primal spirits beyond normal classification.

11 Not to be confused with the 'Covenant of Hallows' which is a derivative rite that serves to commemorate that original and singular pact or appointment, annually, around the Darkest Moon tide closest to All Hallows' Eve. Several principles are shared by these two related rites.

12 In fact we have found that it is Dame Gaude, or Madame la Guiden, who leads the hunt on such occasions, which in light of the act taking place and the dedications later given to the Maid, makes perfect sense.

13 This forms the crux of the belief that a 'witch may not die until their Virtue has been 'passed on.' In this case that of the Clan. Astrologically, there is an event that occurs every 19 years – a conjunction of the Sun and Moon known as the Druidic Great Year. This event forms the actual mythological basis for the general Term of Office for each Virtue holder, accountable retrospectively for 5 generations, one to another in succession.

14 Jones, RiTT. p166

15 not given

16 form not given

17 In the annual commemoration of the 'Rite of All Hallows,' this Covenant is thereafter celebrated in two halves. In the first half, initiated at All Hallows, the Magister leads the 'Pale-Faced Goddess' through the maze across the bridge to descend together into the spiral Mound, taking the cuveenors with them to be among the dead. She is witness to their remembrance through Her and to all

souls of the Clan, past, present and future. The second half completes the 'Rite' at 'Candlemas' when as the 'Fair Child of Compassion,' she re-emerges from the mound and is offered once again the soul candles, affirming their oaths to Her.

18   Of course, even though the reasons for this have since then been much researched, it should still be stressed that a descendent of Cain, who in mistaking his 'grandsire' for a deer, shot him through with an arrow mortally wounding him. An act that aligns the spirit of both hunter and the hunted to the sacrificial victim – all become as one! Importantly, this expresses the continuity of spiritual descent from one to another, often missing one or two generations as Cochrane keenly noted, conceding the cumulative authority of those bound in similar acts of sacrifice preceding them. To some degree this theme is paralleled within Cochrane's own life when claiming his own troubled heritage. Curiously Odhin's spear strikes true, when carried by one pure in heart. And is a powerful symbol of evolution.

19   See appendix 3

20   Known as the 'Cuccilattii'

21   In our modern times, because no literal sacrifice is demanded of the Clan Magister, it represents the lineal descent of 'Sacrificial Virtue' from our original progenitor through the Twin Horn gods into the Magister, his Maid and so on. As each Magister dies, he becomes the 'King of the Castle' and Guardian of the Mound [the hunted]. The new Magister who takes his place becomes the 'Dirty Rascal, the challenger and hunter.' The Roebuck in the Thicket is the Virtue entrapped by that duty of descent, taken by the first 'hunter.' Hence they become as 'one.'

22   Otherwise often referred to as T'owd lad and lass, where names are

unclassified or taboo.

23 Through a mill wheel, would be especially effective.

24 See Appendix 2 (The Pellar)

25 One masculine and three feminine to represent the Horn King and the triune Goddess.

26 As medieval archetypes of the courtly Lover and the Beloved.

27 The Feast of Hekate in fact, who brings life, death and wisdom, reaped and sown in equal measure.

28 Because the Old God was in essence considered to be Lord of manifest things in all their forms, this made perfect sense. The Totem, the Clan leader and the God shared the same essence and were symbolically of the same 'family.' Hence we say, the Hunter, the Hunted (Old Tubal Cain) and the Roebuck in the Thicket are one and the same.

29 The bones serve as a graphic reminder of our fragile mortality, and of the blood and dust of which we are formed upon them. Stripped to this primal image, we gaze into the 'mask' of the Pale-Faced Goddess who at Her appointed time comes for us as the Immortal Beloved with her kiss of death, as celebrated at 'All Hallows.'

30 Jones, RCL p22

31 Sacrament of bread, wine and salt – the Anglo-Saxon term for the Eucharist.

32 Robert Graves described this Lady identically in every detail except the hair which for him was 'bright,' where here the description given by Robert Cochrane is black.

33 Ironically, it is in this realisation that we must then surrender in

order to progress.

34   Tragically, this intent inclines us towards self-destruction and that of others closest to us. In the end we become victims only to ourselves in the nightmare realms of an illusory world constructed from our fractured egos; Robert Cochrane, almost certainly fell prey to this temptation.

35   Everything we do affects us at the soul level of existence; this indents a pattern through the psychic aspects of the self on the physical, mental, and spiritual levels, affecting the karmic resonance in this existence.

36   See appendix 5 for a traditional Roman recipe.

37   E. J. Jones, 'The Robert Cochrane Letters' 2002 Capall Bann UK letter to Bill Gray p140

38   Not because they are secret, but because they are sacred and their gnosis must be an epiphanic act – inside out, not outside in.

39   As in 'prepared'.

40   Of course the eternal divine feminine is truly beyond the three static forms of womanhood she is commonly depicted as being. She is timeless and ageless; She is all encompassing, at once and forever.

41   Jack is of course a euphemism for the Devil himself, and this line refers to the witting surrender of individual will or ego to master one's fate – a seeming paradox.

42   A fourth rite that of the Stone Stile denotes the marking of boundaries, which encompasses the other three within it. Simplest of all, it exhorts the remembrance of the ritual area as a boundary, a peripheral reminder of the sacred usage within it by the Clan across

all three sites.

43 Note Bene: the Three Priestly Mysteries comprised of the Cave (female as seer), the Castle (male as sorcerer) and the Grave (priest as pilgrim/initiate) are not to be confused with the distinctly separate male and female mysteries taught by the Maid and Magister respectively throughout, between and around the knots of the year.

44 ie, those aspirants whom consider themselves prepared to make the shift into the 'godi' foundations of the Faith.

45 The wording of our particular seer chant is not given here. Use a substitute as appropriate.

46 Implying that, in this appended sense, a witch is able to traverse the realms of life, death and beyond quite freely, at will, being the leaper between — essentially 'outside time' ....but the pagan cannot.

47 Similar to the visions of Teresa of Avila regarding her Inner Castles.

48 Here the Stang or Qutub is the emblem of the Old Horned God's power: it becomes the Horse, the magical vehicle par excellence by which we may traverse the realms of the un-manifest to the Source or Void.

49 This will generate Virtue into the "Four square 'Castle' that turns upon the Winds," from whence it makes the shift into eight — the Merkavah, traversing the planes of the hierarchies until the Singularity or Zero point is reached.

50 They have many layers of meaning, being significant to purpose and application.

51 See Appendix 4 for rosary making and meaning.

52 In Luciferian traditions, the red and white roses signify an alchemical

relationship between the soul and spirit represented by the male and female aspects of Lucifer and Sophia- together entwined they generate the golden child of promise, that is the enlightened state of bliss represented by the yellow or golden rose. The Castle is the Body of the Creatrix, the Mind of the individual connected to the 'Other' Castle of the Ancestors.

53 But those who go to explore the Castle of the Goddess that spins without motion between the two worlds, travel North, to Hyperborea.

54 See Appendix 5

55 Of course, any of the above invocations may be replaced and this was John's full intention in presenting this rite in this form, specifically to encourage aspirants to experience some of the lesser known mysteries.

56 And it is not the intention of this editor to break that pattern.

57 As in the sense of 'primality'.

58 One is minded here of Al Khidir, whose vegetal wisdom speaks through his organic mantle.

59 This is in fact based on Anglo-Saxon and Germanic practise, where the sword as a deific symbol [possibly Tiwaz, cognate with Mars] was a popular arbiter. between men in dispute, and for the pronouncement of solemn oaths.

60 http://www.myetymology.com/

61 http://www.myetymology.com

62 http://net.bible.org/lexicon.php?word=expel

63 Gratten & Singer 1952: 151-157

64   R. Kieckhefer, 2000:71

65   V. Flint 1991:270

66   Gratten & Singer, 1952: 175

Index

Other books by Shani Oates

The Arcane Veil: Witchcraft and Occult Science from the People of the Dark-ages to the People of Goda, of the Clan of Tubal Cain.'

Vol One: 978-1-906958-35-0 (£25/$40 hbk)

'analogue of Craft historiography, brought up to date through the author's own experiential praxis'

A discursive investigation of magical beliefs and practises in England since 600CE to the post-modern fall-out of the 21st century, analysing in particular its influences and survival strategies. Emphasis is placed on Christian , Heathen, and Hermetic Praxis, with provocative , critical study of the concepts of Lucifer, Witch-Blood,Sin-Eating and their influences on modern Traditional Craft praxes.

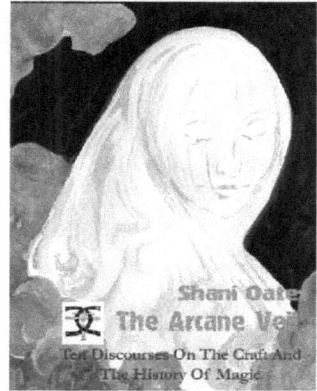

Tubelo's Green Fire: Mythos, Ethos, Female, Male & Priestly Mysteries of the Clan of Tubal Cain By Shani Oates
ISBN 978-1-906958-07-7, £12.99/$23 288pp
Special Edition isbn 978-1-906958 121 £25 /$46
signed by the author (limited availability)

This book explores historical and contemporary ideas of witchcraft through the perspective of the Clan of Tubal Cain - a closed Initiatory group aligned to the Shadow mysteries within the Luciferian stream. As students of arte we mediate the ancestral stream, teaching through practice with the sacred tenets of Truth, Love and Beauty. The Word is thus manifest in deed and vision.

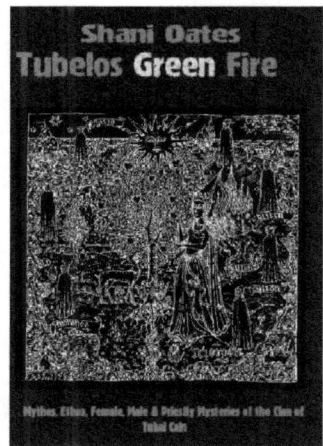

Order direct from
Mandrake of Oxford, PO Box 250, Oxford, OX1 1AP (UK)
Phone: 01865 243671 (for credit card sales)
Prices include economy postage
online at - www.mandrake.uk.net, Email: mandrake@mandrake.uk.net

www.ingramcontent.com/pod-product-compliance
Lightning Source LLC
Chambersburg PA
CBHW060421100426
42812CB00030B/3267/J